NEW YORK SPORTS TRIVIA

Ed Maloney
and
J. Alexander Poulton

OVER TIME BOOKS

The Publisher: OverTime Books is an imprint of Éditions de la Montagne Verte

Library and Archives Canada Cataloguing in Publication

Maloney, Ed, 1961–
    New York sports trivia / Ed Maloney and J. Alexander Poulton.

Includes bibliographical references.
ISBN 978-1-897277-66-9

    1. Sports—New York (State)—Miscellanea.
I. Poulton, J. Alexander (Jay Alexander), 1977– II. Title.

GV584.N7M64 2011   796.09747   C2011-905132-X

Project Director: J. Alexander Poulton
Editor: Jordan Allan
Cover Images: Baseball glove: © Bobbiholmes I Dreamstime.com; football: © Toddtaulman I Dreamstime.com; track sprinter: © Jupiterimages; boxing gloves: © Zedcor Wholly Owned; golfer: © iStockphoto.com I Sergey Kashkin; basketball hoop: © 2011 Thinkstock; volleyball: © 2007 iStock Photo I Andres Peiro Palmer; football helmet: © 2007 iStock Photo I Jason Lugo: Yankee Stadium: © 2010 Nathalia Guaus I Dreamstime.com; New Meadowlands Stadium: © 2008 Jmad I Dreamstime.com; Madison Square Garden: © 2009 Paskee I Dreamstime.com; all other photos: © Photos.com

We acknowledge the financial support of the Government of Canada through the Canada Book Fund (CBF) for our publishing activities.

Government of Québec—Tax Credit for book publishing—Administered by SODEC

SODEC
Québec ✚✚

 Canadian   Patrimoine
Heritage   canadien

PC: 1

Contents

Dedication

To Arthur Maloney, Kathryn Ryan, Denis O'Shea and Juliana Cronin. A century ago they left behind their families and friends in the Emerald Isle to pursue their hopes and dreams in the New World. And to their children, especially Edward Maloney and Patricia O'Shea; my siblings Mary, Kathleen and Richard; and my godmother, Margret-Ann Maloney, whose sacrifice, love, devotion and encouragement have allowed me to pursue mine.

– Ed Maloney

To James Mongeluzo

– J. Alexander Poulton

Acknowledgments

I was a child when I left the care of Dr. Ramon Castroviejo and Dr. Carlos Uribe, two pioneers in the field of cornea research. Thanks to their dedication to their vocation 50 years ago, I have the gift of sight.

I've also benefited from the professionalism, mentoring and friendship of scores of individuals in my career as a writer, editor and online producer, especially at *Newsday*, *The Ring* magazine and CBS SportsLine. My eternal thanks to Mike Acri, John and Maureen Andrias, Bill Apter, Steve Aronowitz, Dotty Beekman, Al Bello, Ed Brophy, Jeff Brophy, Arlen D. "Spider" Bynum, Mike Candel, Leon Carter, Bob Cassidy, Eric Compton, Dan Donneghy, Jon Duero, Steve Farhood, Joe Feeney, Geraldine Gillespie, Ken Gillespie, Jack Hartigan, Thomas Hayes, Mark Herrmann, Stan Isaacs, John Jeansonne, Dave Kaplan, Hank Kaplan, Joe Kelly, John Q. Kelly, Margret-Ann Kelly, Jack Lambert, Mary Lambert, Patrick Lappin Sr., Patrick Lappin Jr., Gil Lilienthal, Greg Logan, Ed McNamara, Ray McNeil, Sheila McNeil, Don Majeski, Linda Maleski, Arthur Maloney, PhD, Kathryn Maloney, Captain Richard J. Maloney (FDNY, Ret.), John Maloney, Wanda Maloney, Connie Mango, Steve Marcus, Steve Matthews, Wallace Matthews, Kevin Mattimore, Tony Mauro, Arthur Mercante Sr., Gerry Monigan, Larry Murray, Mary Murray, Robert O'Neill, Craig Peters, John Quinn, Francis Romano, Dave Rubinstein, Evan Rudowski,

Jeff Ryan, Stu Saks, Bob Smith, Jim Smith, Pete Tamburello, Manny Topol, John Truehart and George Usher.

A tip of the hat goes to Joe Pauly, and Frank and Denise Maloney for their critique and review of early versions of the manuscript. And I am extremely grateful for the professionalism and dedication of the editorial staff at OverTime Books. Because of my love of sports and history, I knew this assignment would be extremely rewarding—I was not disappointed.

– Ed Maloney

Introduction

I knew when I took this assignment that the hard part would not be choosing what events and personalities to write about, but what and who to edit out once all the research was done. I grew up among family members, friends and other acquaintances who were old enough to have rooted for the New York "baseball" Giants, the Yankees before Babe Ruth and a heavyweight boxing champion named Jack Dempsey.

"Sports didn't begin with Mickey Mantle and Muhammad Ali," I was once informed in a very patronizing manner. With that in mind, I came to appreciate that the world of sports doesn't revolve around New York City. Indeed, from Binghamton to Buffalo, New Yorkers and New York's other pro sports teams, not to mention colleges and universities and both amateur and professional athletes, have left their marks in the world of sports as well as the nation and around the globe.

Cynics claim that athletic competition doesn't build character, but I disagree. You'll see in the stories of the people and events in the pages that follow that it wasn't all about wins and losses—at its best, competitive sports *reveal* character. This book is not a history of sports in the Empire State or of its great athletes, nor does it attempt to be. Rather, it's a collection of facts and anecdotes with some bits and pieces of uncommon knowledge that we hope you find as much fun to read as we did to discover during our research and writing. Even though we call it "trivia," it's hardly trivial.

Chapter One

The Birthplace and Showcase of Baseball

Doubleday Double-cross

The origins of many professional sports are clouded in mystery, and baseball's history is no exception. Cooperstown, the home of the National Baseball Hall of Fame and Museum, is widely believed to be the birthplace of baseball and is where Abner Doubleday laid out the first baseball diamond in 1839. This story, however, is false. The Doubleday myth spread easily because it centered on a man who later became a Civil War hero and who later achieved greater fame through many published articles. But just as the Doubleday story claimed to be the genesis of baseball, many other pretenders surfaced over the years as well. To settle the debate once and for all, a special commission funded by Spalding, a leading sporting goods company, was set up in 1905 and aimed to prove that the game was invented in the United States.

During its investigation, the commission received a letter from a man claiming to corroborate the Doubleday origin story. In the letter, the man claimed that he was a childhood friend of Doubleday and that Doubleday had scratched the plans for the new game in the dust of a field in Cooperstown. But the commission quickly disproved the man's claims because at the time of the alleged incident, the man would have been just five years old when Doubleday was 20. Plus, Doubleday himself never even mentioned this new sport he was supposed to have invented in any of the articles and letters he wrote later in life. At the end of the commission's investigation, they failed to answer the question as to the origin of the game and in the end only served to further confuse the annals of sports history by giving voice to a variety of bogus stories. So the Doubleday myth continued as the most likely and the most relatable story to baseball fans.

The truth of the matter is that New Yorker Alexander J. Cartwright wrote down the modern rules of the game in 1845, and they were first used in a game in New York between the Gothhams and the Knickerbockers. The facts are there for the world to see but still the Doubleday myth persists, proving fiction is sometimes easier to believe than fact. Still, baseball was definitely created in New York, and New Yorkers remain baseball's greatest practitioners.

The Strange Origin of Shin Guards

For some players, it would be impossible to imagine playing baseball without shin guards, but as practical an invention as they might seem, their origins are steeped in America's dark history of racial intolerance and bigotry. During the 1880s, the minor league's

International League was open to black players, but the white players' attitudes toward them were not. It was no secret that many white players on opposing teams tried to blatantly injure the black players.

Two black second basemen knew this fact more than anyone. Binghamton's Bud Fowler and Buffalo's Frank Grant knew that every time white opponents tried to steal their base, they would purposely slide in with their spikes aimed directly at their shins. So Fowler and Grant came up with the idea of wrapping wooden slats around their shins in order to stop the spikes from tearing up their legs. Their solution worked for a few games, but once the opposing white players learned of their makeshift defense, they began to sharpen their spikes to pierce through the thin wooden slats. As a result of the assaults, many black players moved to the outfield. And it is because of this racial hatred that baseball players around the world now wear shin guards in every game, nowadays made from reinforced plastic so no spikes can get through.

New York Giants

The Toasts of the Town

As hard as it is to believe, there was a time when the Yankees were New York's afterthought baseball franchise. In the first two decades of the 20th century, the top gate attraction in the Big Apple was the New York Giants. Their manager was John McGraw, and the team was owned by one of the most powerful and influential men in sports, John T. Brush. The Giants owner wielded enough influence that he canceled the 1904 World Series because of a feud with the American League's founder and president Ban Johnson. The Fall Classic resumed the next year but only after Brush gave his approval.

Brush built the Polo Grounds, which became the state-of-the-art sports arena in America. With the colorful McGraw managing the team, and the game's most popular player, Christy Mathewson, on the mound, the Giants consistently ranked among baseball's top teams, and they were easily the best team in New York. From 1903 to 1925, the Giants—you didn't need to say "baseball Giants"—finished first or second 19 times, won nine pennants and three World Series.

Six decades after the team left for San Francisco, the only relic that remained in the Polo Grounds was a staircase that was built in 1913 and dedicated to Brush, who died November 26, 1912. It is in such disrepair and overgrown with brush that many people in the neighborhood don't even know it exists. The John T. Brush Memorial Staircase led from the bluff behind the grounds, which was demolished in 1964, down to where the ticket booths were, near the entrance behind home plate. As part of the city's historical project, it was decided that the staircase should be repaired. The Yankees, Mets, football Giants and Jets donated funds for the renovation. And in homage to the team's rich past, the ownership in San Francisco did as well. The Giants may have left, but their glorious legacy remains.

The First Mr. October

The New York Giants won their second straight National League pennant in 1905. And with the differences between the two leagues resolved, the World Series was resumed after a one-year hiatus. The American League champion Philadelphia Athletics faced a six-man pitching staff whose five starters totaled 115 complete games. They all had winning records, and none had an ERA over 2.87. Manager John McGraw's ace was 24-year-old Christy Mathewson (31–9, 1.28 ERA), who had just won 30 games for the second straight year. The "Big Six," as Mathewson was called, was tabbed to start the opener on October 9, 1905, in Philadelphia.

In game one, "Matty" gave the A's fits, scattering four hits over nine innings in a 3–0 Giants win. Philadelphia won game two in New York by the same score to even the series at one game apiece. Mathewson took the mound again for game three on October 12 and threw another four-hit shutout as New York won easily, 9–0. The Giants took a 3–1 lead in the best-of-seven series when future Hall of Famer Joe McGinnity went the distance in a 1–0 victory at the Polo Grounds. With Philadelphia struggling to score runs, McGraw went back to his ace for game five in New York on October 14. Once again, Matty held the A's in check, allowing only five hits as the Giants won the championship with a 2–0 win. In the span of just six days, Mathewson threw three complete-game shutouts. In his three victories, the future Hall of Famer allowed just 13 hits and walked one batter.

The Big Six remains the greatest pitcher in Giants history—New York or San Francisco—and one of the greatest in the annals of Major League Baseball. He retired with a career record of 373–188 and a 2.13 ERA. McGraw's go-to guy won 20 or more games 13 times, including every season from 1903 to 1914. Four times in that span, he won more than 30 games. Mathewson didn't pitch again in the World Series until 1911, where the Giants once again faced Philadelphia. This time, the A's got to Matty for six hits and actually scored a run in the second inning but still lost the opener 2–1. Mathewson had not allowed a run in a record 28⅓ innings.

He pitched in a total of four Fall Classics, with the Giants on the losing end three times. He was 5–5 in the 11 games that he started, finishing 10 of them, throwing 101 innings and allowing just 11 runs for a 0.97 ERA. Mathewson's scoreless innings streak record would last just seven years. It was broken by a young left-handed pitcher on the Boston Red Sox, who set a new mark of 29⅔ innings without allowing a run—that southpaw's name was Babe Ruth.

A Colossal Collapse

McGraw's crew won three consecutive pennants from 1911 to 1913, but each season ended on a sour note with a loss in the World Series. Nothing, however, could prepare the team for the disappointment of how the 1914 season ended. Although Mathewson and Rube Marquard appeared to be off their games that season, the team looked to be cruising along to its fourth straight pennant. A win over the Pirates on

July 25 extended their winning streak to six games and left the Giants in first place with a 51–32 record.

The outlook for the remainder of the season couldn't have looked bleaker for the Boston Braves. A week earlier on July 17, the last-place Braves arrived in Cincinnati 10 games below .500 (33–43) and 11.5 games behind the Giants. Rallying behind starting pitchers Bill James (26–7, 1.90 ERA) and Dick Rudolph (26–10, 2.35 ERA), manager George Stallings guided the Tribe to a 61–16 record the rest of the way to win the flag with a 94–59 ledger, besting second-place New York. The Giants, who were 58–40 with a 6.5 lead as late as August 12, went 26–30 down the stretch and finished 10.5 games behind Boston at 84–70.

A Record Streak to Nowhere

On September 7, 1916, the New York Giants beat the visiting Brooklyn Robins 4–1 at the Polo Grounds and began a record 26-game winning streak. In the course of the streak, they defeated every team in the National League. The only bump in their road came when they tied the Pittsburgh Pirates 1–1. Earlier that May, manager John McGraw's boys won 17 in a row. Unfortunately, the rest of the year they went 43–66, which accounts for their fourth-place finish at the end of the season.

Bad Day at the Office

Professional athletes make mistakes. That is a given. Errors are a part of baseball, and even the greatest have had bad days on the field, but nothing in the history of the game can compare to 1895 New York Giants third baseman Mike Grady making four errors on a single play! So here's how the bad plays added up:

1. On a routine ground ball, Grady threw over to first but missed the mark completely, sending it over the first baseman's head.

2. The first baseman then retrieved the ball and threw it back to Grady to prevent the runner from reaching third, but Grady missed the ball for his second error.

3. Following the ball into the dugout, Grady picked it up and tried to get the runner at home, but his attempt sailed over the head of the catcher for error number three.

4. The error led to the runner scoring, which marked Grady for a fourth error on one play. The runner, in the meantime, had himself one of the strangest inside-the-park home runs ever.

Terry: A Forgotten Hero

If you had to guess which New York, or even San Francisco, Giant had the highest career batting average, you might guess Willie Mays, Barry Bonds or even Mel Ott—but you'd be wrong. One of the greatest and perhaps most underappreciated players in the history of New York baseball is Giants first baseman and manager Bill Terry.

Born in 1898, Terry began playing pro ball when he was just 16. But the Atlanta native didn't make it to the big leagues until 1923, and it took him two more seasons before he broke into the starting lineup. Once he did, Terry hit .310 or better in 11 of his final 12 seasons. He had more than 200 hits in six seasons, including a record 254 in 1930. That same year, Terry led all hitters in the major leagues with a .401 batting average. He is the last National League player to top .400 in a season.

Terry played on three pennant winners, including the Giants championship team of 1933 when he was a player-manager. The man who was dubbed "Memphis Bill" was so highly thought of that he was chosen to succeed John McGraw as manager during the 1932 season. Terry retired as a player in 1936 and managed the Giants until 1941. They won the pennant again in 1937 but lost 4–2 in the World Series to the Yankees. Terry's .341 lifetime batting average is the highest of any National League player who batted left handed, and he was elected into the Hall of Fame in 1954.

Hubbell Fans Six Future Famers

The Hall of Fame trustees at Cooperstown had no problem filling Carl Hubbell's plaque with career highlights when he was inducted in 1947. Hubbell had a career record of 253–154 and won at least 21 games from 1933 to 1937. "King Carl" led the National League three times in victories and earned run average during that time, and he won the National League MVP in 1933 and 1936. His 24 consecutive victories that spanned from 1936 to 1937 remain a record. But the first of his impressive feats listed was his still unequaled pitching performance in the 1934 All-Star game.

As the starting pitcher in front of a hometown crowd at the Polo Grounds, Hubbell showed the best American Leaguers what batters on the senior circuit had to endure. After allowing a single to leadoff hitter Charlie Gehringer of the Tigers and a walk to Heinie Marnush of the Senators, Hubbell struck out, in this order: Babe Ruth, Lou Gehrig and Philadelphia's Jimmie Foxx. King Carl opened the second inning by striking out Philadelphia's Al Simmons and Boston's Joe Cronin before Yankee catcher Bill Dickey singled. Hubbell then fanned American League starter Lefty Gomez of the Yankees to retire the side. Hubbell humbled five consecutive future Hall of Fame players, and at that time Ruth, Gehrig and Foxx were the top three power hitters in the game.

Ott's Blast Gives the Giants the Series

In 1933, the Giants won the National League pennant and returned to the World Series for the first time in nine years. It was their first under new player-manager Bill Terry. Led by pitcher Carl Hubbell and their slugging right fielder Mel Ott, the Giants beat the Washington Senators, 4–1. Ott hit .389, with two home runs, the second of which was a solo shot that broke a 3–3 tie in the bottom of the 10th inning of the deciding game five to give New York the win. It was the first time the World Series had ended on a home run. Hubbell dominated on the mound, pitching two complete-game victories without allowing an earned run over 20 innings.

The Bicoastal Curse Ends

Many athletes and their fans are superstitious. They swear by pregame routines, wearing special articles of clothing or partaking in certain rituals on game day. If you doubt the validity of a supernatural connection in sports, just ask fans of the Boston Red Sox and Chicago Cubs. Up until recently, San Francisco baseball fans wondered what sort of unlucky hex had been put on their Giants. The team had not won a championship since they left New York in 1957. Some fans with a deep knowledge of the team's history believe that the curse of Edward L. Grant stood between them and the World Series trophy.

The college-educated Grant, or "Harvard Eddie" as he was called, was a journeyman player who was known for using correct grammar on the field. For example, he would scream "I have it!" as opposed to "I got it!" during a career from 1905 to 1915 with the Indians and Giants. Grant joined the army during World War I. Five weeks before the Armistice was signed, Grant was killed in action. He was one of the most prominent Americans who died in the Great War. On Memorial Day 1921, representatives from the armed forces, Major League Baseball and Grant's family unveiled a five-foot-high monument in center field at the Polo Grounds in New York, paying tribute to Captain Edward L. Grant. Over the years, the plaque became the focal point of Memorial Day events at the Polo Grounds.

The monument was well known to players, who passed it every day (the clubhouses at the Polo Grounds were located in centerfield), as well as to the fans, who were allowed to leave the stadium through the centerfield exit after games. The Grant monument can be seen to the left of the screen at the beginning of the highlight film of Willie Mays' memorable catch off Vic Wertz in the 1954 World Series. After the Giants final game in New York, Grant's plaque was stolen and then later recovered, but eventually disappeared for good. In 2001, according to the Great War Society and the Western Front Association, they approached Giants ownership with an offer to replace the plaque honoring Eddie Grant at SBC Park in San Francisco. The Giants declined the offer.

The following season, San Francisco, who led the Angels 3–2 after five games, blew a lead in game six and also eventually game seven of the World Series. The next year, the Giants were upset in the first round of the divisional playoffs by the prohibitive underdog Florida Marlins, when Jose Cruz Jr. dropped a fly ball in the 11th inning of the pivotal game three. Finally, in 2006, the Giants agreed to honor Grant and erected a replica of the plaque that now hangs near an elevator at the Lefty O'Doul entrance gate at the AT&T Park.

On the team's next trip to the World Series, the Giants beat the Texas Rangers for their first championship in 56 years. More importantly, San Francisco management realized that the memory of this former player deserved to be acknowledged even if he was a member of the team decades before it relocated. After all, Edward L. Grant was not only, as the bronze plaque on the monument reads, a "Soldier, Scholar, Athlete," he was also a Giant.

Stoneham Gets a Pass, But Why?

Despite winning the National League pennant in 1951 and the World Series in 1954, by the mid-1950s the Giants had become the third team in a three-team town. The Dodgers now dominated the National League, winning six pennants from 1947 to 1956, and the Yankees, situated just across the Harlem River in the Bronx, were the perennial kings of baseball. By 1955, the Giants attendance was falling and crime in the area around the Polo Grounds was rising.

Giants owner Horace Stoneham watched while his counterpart with the Dodgers, Walter O'Malley, haggled with city officials to get a new stadium in Brooklyn. The Braves had recently moved from Boston to Milwaukee, about one-tenth the size of New York, and were drawing more than two million fans to home games while fewer than half as many journeyed to Coogan's Bluff to watch the Giants. The Giants drew 1,155,067 to the Polo Grounds in 1954, when they won their last championship. Two years later, attendance had dropped to just 629,179. It wasn't much better in 1957, their last in New York, when 653,923 showed up for their 67 home dates, an average of 9760 in a park with a capacity of 54,555.

Stoneham, who was 33 when he assumed ownership of the team upon the death of his father in 1936, was in negotiations with Minneapolis when O'Malley introduced him to San Francisco city officials in 1956.

Baseball owners were more inclined to approve O'Malley's move to Los Angeles as long as there were two teams situated on the West Coast. Stoneham and the City of San Francisco reached an agreement, and the Giants' move to the City by the Bay was finalized in the fall of 1957.

Meanwhile, O'Malley, who told Los Angeles officials that he'd rather stay in New York if a deal could finally be reached with Big Apple politicians, accepted Los Angeles' offer when the season was over. While Giants fans were heartbroken that the team was leaving, whatever negative sentiments they had toward Stoneham didn't compare to the rabid hatred Brooklynites held, and still hold, for Walter O'Malley.

Brooklyn Dodgers

Brooklyn Falls to BoSox in World Series

After contending for a few seasons, the Brooklyn Robins—they didn't officially change their name to Dodgers until 1932—made their first appearance in the World Series in 1916, which they lost 4–1 to the Boston Red Sox. A highlight of that year's Fall Classic was the game-two pitching duel between starting pitchers Sherry Smith and Boston's 21-year-old lefty, Babe Ruth.

Centerfielder Hi Myers staked the Robins to a 1–0 lead with a solo inside-the-park home run in the top of the first. Boston tied the score in the bottom of the third when Everett Scott tripled and scored on Ruth's ground out to second base. Nobody else scored until the bottom of the 14th inning. Boston first baseman

Dick Hoblitzell worked Smith for a walk and advanced to second on a sacrifice. Hoblitzell was then taken out for pinch runner Mike McNally, who came around to score on pinch hitter Gainer's single to left field to give the Red Sox a 2–1 win.

Both teams had their chances to score. The Robins had six hits and three walks off Ruth, while the Red Sox managed seven hits and three walks off Smith. It's worth noting that Ruth didn't allow a hit after the eighth inning. The 13 scoreless innings Ruth threw following Myers first-inning home run started a then-record streak that reached 29⅔ scoreless innings in the World Series. The record was eventually broken by Yankee southpaw Whitey Ford, who stranded runners for 32⅓ innings in the late '50s and early '60s.

Smith missed the season in 1918 and part of 1919 because of military service in World War I. He appeared in two games for the Dodgers in the 1920 World Series and allowed just one earned run in 17 innings, but Brooklyn still fell 5–2 to Cleveland. Smith retired following the 1927 season with a mediocre 114–118 career record, but in the World Series, he was 1–2 and allowed only three earned runs in 30⅓ innings for a staggering 0.89 ERA. Smith, at least in World Series play, edges Dodger legend Sandy Kofax, who boasted a 0.95 ERA over 57 innings.

A Marathon Battle of Wits and Arms

The Robins came to Boston on the last day of April 1920 in second place, one game behind the Reds. They dropped the series opener 3–0 on what was the final day of Standard Time. That game took one hour, 33 minutes to play. Saturday, May 1, was the first day of Daylight Savings Time in Boston that year, and it couldn't have come soon enough as the Robins sent right-hander Leon Cadore against Boston's Joe Oeschger.

Brooklyn's scoreless streak against Braves pitching ended in the top of the fifth inning when second baseman Ivy Olsen drove in catcher Ernie Kruger to give the Robins a 1–0 lead. It was Olsen's only hit in 10 at bats that day. Cadore's "cushion" ended an inning later when Boston right fielder Walton Cruise tripled and scored on third baseman Tony Boeckel's single. And that's the way it stayed until umpire Barry McCormick called the game three hours, 50 minutes later on account of darkness after a record 26 innings. Both teams pleaded for at least another inning, but the ump refused and the game went into the record books as a 1–1 tie. After all, it's not as if they didn't have their chances to win it. Despite getting to Cadore for 15 hits and five walks, Boston left 17 men on base. Oeschger scattered nine hits, walked four and left 11 men stranded.

Although many sports writers felt the marathon outing by the two pitchers would ruin their careers, both men pitched several more seasons. Oeschger turned in a career best 20–14 year in 1921. It's worth noting that Cadore didn't pitch again until May 21, and it appears the time off did him some good. Against the first-place Reds in Cincinnati, the right-hander went the distance—this time only nine innings, luckily—and allowed just six hits in a 3–0 win.

Would Somebody Score, Please!

Boston hosted Brooklyn again on Monday afternoon, May 3, 1920, as the teams took to Braves Field to close out the three-game series. What transpired on that day was almost as impressive as Saturday's contest. If you sent this one to Ripley's *Believe It Or Not*, they'd send it back. No way! Not two games in a row!

Brooklyn sent Sherry Smith to the mound, and the Braves countered with Dana Fillingim. Once again, Brooklyn struck first as Smith, who went 2-for-8, scored the Robins only run in the fifth inning. Boston tied the score in the bottom of the sixth. Like Cadore and Oeschger two days earlier, Smith and Fillingim locked horns and made life miserable for batters over the next few hours. Meanwhile, there was no action in either bullpen. With the sun setting, the players, the umpiring crew and what was left of the 3500 who were on hand when the game began, started to wonder if the contest would also end in a tie. But with one out in the bottom of the 19th, Boston finally scored for the 2–1 win. Needless to say, the Robins looked forward to a change of venue. Not only were they swept by the Braves, but they also scored just two runs in 54 innings in the three games in Boston.

Dazzy Left 'Em Dazzled

Charles Arthur "Dazzy" Vance was Major League Baseball's ultimate late bloomer. The Orient, Iowa, native was born in 1891 and, with the exception two brief stints with the Pirates and Yankees, spent a decade in the minor leagues before joining the Dodgers as a starting pitcher in 1922 at age 31. Vance won 18 games in both 1922 and 1923 and led the National League in strikeouts both years.

Then came his career season of 1924. The 6-foot-2, 200-pound right-hander led the majors with 28 wins (versus six losses), 262 strikeouts and a 2.16 ERA, and he was voted National League Most Valuable Player. In an August game against the Cubs, he set a then-record of 15 strikeouts for a nine-inning game. A month later, the Cubs were part of another career highlight when Vance struck out three batters on nine pitches in the second inning of Brooklyn's win over Chicago.

Vance was almost as good in 1925. He led all big league pitchers in wins (22) and strikeouts (221), and once again the Cubs were used as foils. In July, Vance fanned 17 Chicago batters in a 4–3 win. Another milestone occurred on September 13 when he hurled a no-hitter, with just one walk and nine strikeouts, against the Phillies at Ebbets Field.

Vance was the National League strikeout king from 1922 to 1928; five of those seven seasons he led the majors. His 262 total in 1924 was more than the combined total of teammate Burleigh Grimes, who was second with 135, and Cincinnati's Dolf Luque, who was third with 86. That season, Vance had one out of every 13 strikeouts in the entire National League. His third and final 20-game season came in 1928—he went 22–10 and led the majors in ERA (2.09) and strikeouts (200). He pitched for Brooklyn through 1932. He spent the 1933 and 1934 seasons with the Cardinals and Reds before rejoining Brooklyn, where he retired following the 1935 campaign at age 44. He was elected into the Hall of Fame in 1955.

A Brief, But Memorable, Career

Brooklyn outfielder Al Gionfriddo was a key player in two major plays of the 1947 World Series between the Dodgers and the Yankees; the latter remains one of the most famous plays in World Series history. The journeyman outfielder, who played a total of 228 games over three years with the Pirates and one with the Dodgers, entered game four as a pinch runner for Carl Furillo in the bottom of the ninth inning at Ebbets Field.

With two outs and the Dodgers trailing 2–1, Gionfriddo stole second. Yankee pitcher Bill Bevans then intentionally walked Pete Reiser. Bevans had not allowed a hit up to that point, but Reiser was the 10th Dodger to reach base on a walk. Dodger manager Burt Shotten then sent in Eddie Miksis to pinch run for Reiser. Bevans now faced Cookie Lavagetto, who was pinch hitting for Eddie Stanky. Lavagetto stroked the ball into the right-field corner for a double. Outfielder Tommy Henrich had a problem picking the ball up, and Gionfriddo and Miksis scored on the play to give Brooklyn a 3–2 win and to even the series at two games apiece.

Two games later at Yankee Stadium, Gionfriddo was in left field in the bottom of the seventh inning when Joe DiMaggio belted a shot to deep left center-field. Gionfriddo took off and sprinted to try to make the catch. Dodger broadcaster Red Barber's radio call of the play is as famous as the catch itself: "Swung on, belted!…It's a long one!…Deep into left-center…Back goes Gionfriddo. Back-back-back-back-back-back, heeeeee makes a one-handed catch against the bullpen! Whoa, doctor!" It was the signature play of Gionfriddo's brief career. It's worth noting that for Gionfriddo, Stanky and Bevans, 1947 was their last season in the major leagues.

A Significant Piece to the Puzzle

When Dodger GM Branch Rickey signed Jackie Robinson to a major league contract, some veteran players who had spent their prime years in the Negro leagues groused that Robinson was not the best of the black players. Nevertheless, he was among that league's best players, and more importantly, he was a versatile player who could start at several positions. Aside from signing Robinson, Rickey was in the midst of putting together one of the greatest teams in baseball history. Robinson was Major League Baseball's Rookie of the Year in 1947, he hit .300 six times and was the National League's Most Valuable Player in 1949. He was a great player on a great team.

From 1946 to 1956, Brooklyn won six National League pennants and one World Series, and twice they lost an end-of-season playoff series when they finished the regular season tied for first place.

Two months after the Dodgers lost the 1956 World Series to the Yankees, Robinson was part of a six-player trade with the cross-town Giants in what turned out to be both teams' last season in New York. But at age 37 and his once great skills eroded, Robinson elected to retire.

Greatness Delayed

It's hard to determine how many years Jackie Robinson lost because of Major League Baseball's ban on black baseball players. He certainly would have lost at least three seasons because of military service during World War II. But based on the extraordinary ability he displayed in college—he was the first athlete to earn letters in four sports at UCLA—he probably would have made it to the majors before America entered the war in 1942. Even before he enrolled in college, Robinson was selected to a regional baseball All-Star team in 1938 that featured future Hall of Famers Ted Williams and Bob Lemon.

Robinson's Ship Comes In—and Leaves

As the result of financial difficulties, Jackie Robinson left UCLA without getting his degree in the fall of 1941 to play semi-pro football for the Honolulu Bears. After a short season, Robinson headed back to California. His departure couldn't have come at a better time. On Friday, December 5, he boarded the ocean liner *Lurline* and set sail for home. The ship was half way to California on Sunday morning when the Japanese attacked Pearl Harbor.

Robinson Displayed Versatility

Among the significant accomplishments listed on Jackie Robinson's Hall of Fame plaque are his excellent fielding percentage and the four times he led the league in double plays as a second baseman. Indeed, he has been selected on many all-time teams as a second baseman. But few people know that when Robinson was called up to the Dodgers in 1947, he spent the entire season as Brooklyn's starting first baseman. He didn't shift to second base until 1948.

All in the Family

Greatness on the world stage of sports, and courage and integrity off it, was a part of the Robinson family DNA. Jackie's older brother, Matthew "Mack" Robinson won a silver medal in the 200-meter dash at the 1936 Summer Olympics in Berlin, finishing second to Jesse Owens. When he returned home, Mack enrolled at the University of Oregon, where he earned All-America honors in track before graduating in 1941. Mack returned home to Pasadena and worked for the city. He earned distinction as an advocate against street crime. The city of Pasadena honored the Robinson brothers with a memorial in 1997. Two years later, Pasadena City College named its athletic stadium "Robinson Stadium" after the siblings. And in 2000, the U.S. Postal Service named the new post office in Pasadena the Matthew "Mack" Robinson Post Office Building.

They Made Him an Offer He Couldn't Refuse

A well-known joke among jilted Dodger fans in the years after the team left Brooklyn went something like this: "If Hitler, Stalin and Walter O'Malley were in a room and you had only two bullets, who would you shoot?" The answer: "O'Malley—TWICE!"

The common thought was that O'Malley, who had been part owner of the team since the mid-1940s and became the majority owner in 1950, had cut and run on loyal fans. But nothing could be farther from the truth. O'Malley, a second-generation New Yorker, began expressing his desire in public for a new stadium for the Dodgers as early as 1947. O'Malley wanted to purchase the land as well as finance the building of a new stadium privately. A visionary 20 years ahead of his time, O'Malley envisioned a 50,000-seat dome to be built in Brooklyn. The Houston Astrodome, a similar-style stadium, did not open until 1965.

Ebbets Field, which opened in 1913, held less than 35,000, while the Polo Grounds, home of the Giants, had a capacity of more than 50,000 and Yankee Stadium could accommodate crowds in the mid-60,000 range. So was it that irrational for O'Malley to want a bigger stadium to replace one that was more than 40 years old? The owner even commissioned architecture firms to design and do renderings of a domed stadium and had feasibility studies done over the next 10 years. But he could never get the city of New York to sell him the parcels of land that he needed to build the new stadium.

City and Parks Commissioner Robert Moses wanted O'Malley to move the team to Flushing Meadows, where the legendary Parks Department guru envisioned a multi-sports complex on the site where Shea Stadium and the U.S. Tennis Center were eventually built. But the city would have owned the stadium, and the Dodgers would have been the primary tenants.

In 1954, the City of Los Angeles contacted every Major League Baseball team and pitched the City of Angels as their new home. O'Malley still had not committed to moving the team even as the Dodgers played their last game in Brooklyn at the close of the 1957 season. He told Los Angeles city officials in early October 1957 that he would rather stay in New York if he could get the deal he was seeking. But once the LA city council voted to *give* O'Malley 300 acres to build his privately financed stadium, not to mention the city would also pay for the construction of access roads, the owner agreed to move the team. If O'Malley was truly the avaricious scum that he has been portrayed as for the past five decades, he certainly put on quite a charade from 1947 to 1957. People ignore the fact that, even when the move became a very real possibility in the spring of 1957, New York officials failed to proffer a deal to keep either the Dodgers or Giants.

New York Mets

The Grande Dame of New York Sports

There is really no other way to describe Mrs. Joan Payson, the first owner of the Mets. Mrs. Payson, who was born in 1903, was the daughter of multi-millionaire Payne Whitney and granddaughter of William Collins Whitney, a wealthy and influential financier who at one point served as secretary of the navy in the administration of President Grover Cleveland. Joan's bloodlines on her mother's side were equally impressive. Her mother, Helen Julia Hay, was the daughter of John Hay, a diplomat who had been a presidential assistant to Abraham Lincoln and secretary of state for presidents McKinley and Roosevelt.

Born to a family of wealth and privilege, young Joan shared her mother's love of sports, and the two women were fans of John McGraw's Giants as well as thoroughbred horse racing. Joan and her brother, John, inherited Greentree Stables from their parents and became successful horse breeders themselves. Greentree Stable of Red Bank, New Jersey, and the Greentree breeding farm of Lexington, Kentucky, became major players in horse racing, and they eventually boasted a total of seven winners of thoroughbred horse racing's Triple Crown races: twice in the Kentucky Derby, once in Preakness Stakes and four times in Belmont Stakes.

In 1924, Joan married Charles Shipman Payson, a graduate of Harvard Law School. Mrs. Payson became quite the philanthropist, raising funds for hospitals and universities, and she was also a patron of the arts, with an impressive collection of artwork that can still be viewed at the Metropolitan Museum of Art. After World War II, she became a minority shareowner of her beloved Giants and was the only member of the board of directors to oppose Horace Stoneham's plan to move the team to San Francisco. When Stoneham's motion was approved, Payson sold her interest in the Giants.

Payson then committed herself to bringing a National League franchise back to the city. She convinced Casey Stengel, who was unceremoniously fired by the Yankees two years earlier, to be the manager of her expansion team. "I just couldn't say no to her," said the future Hall of Fame manager. "She was that kind of lady." And in 1962, the Mets took the field at the Polo Grounds, where they played until Shea Stadium was opened two years later. Joan Payson was the first and, other than Marge Schott who owned the Cincinnati Reds from 1984 to 1999, only woman to buy a professional sports team in America.

Although she was born to a life of privilege, Mrs. Payson saw herself as just another enthusiastic fan of the sport and the team that she loved. Instead of the trappings of a secluded owner's box, Mets fans could see Payson at home games in her familiar box seats near the team's dugout, eating hot dogs and ice cream with her grandchildren, keeping score and gladly signing autographs for fans. She remained optimistic during the team's humble, and at times embarrassing, start as management slowly assembled the pieces needed for a championship team.

One of the few times Payson injected herself into the players' personal matters came in 1972 when she helped engineer the acquisition of one of her long-lost Giants. All of New York was grateful when Willie Mays, the "Say Hey Kid," returned home. The Mets won two National League pennants and one memorable World Series during Mrs. Payson's ownership, which lasted until she died in 1975 at age 72. Her children eventually sold off the Mets and Greentree Stable. Joan Whitney Payson is fondly remembered by all of those whose lives she touched and enriched. She left behind a legacy of dignity, generosity and class.

Mets Streak to First Win

On April 23, 1962, the expansion New York Mets finally won their first regular-season game. The Mets record stood at 0–9 after dropping the first two games against the Pirates at Forbes Field in Pittsburgh. But in this game, Felix Mantilla and Elio Chacon got three hits apiece and starting pitcher Jay Hook threw a complete-game as the Mets beat the Pirates 9–1. Coincidentally, the Pirates had opened the season by winning 10 straight games before losing to, of all teams, the Mets.

It was a trying year for New York's newest franchise as they finished with a record of 40–120, which to this day remains the worst record in baseball history. Author Jimmy Breslin best summed up the plight of the early Mets in his 1963 book *Can't Anybody Here Play This Game?:*

> *You see, the Mets are losers, just like nearly every-*
> *body else in life. This is the team for the cab driver*
> *who gets held up and the guy who loses out on*
> *a promotion because he didn't maneuver himself to*

*lunch with the boss enough. It is the team for every
guy who has to get out of bed in the morning and go
to work for short money on a job he does not like.
The Yankees? Who does well enough to root for
them, Laurance Rockefeller?*

Early Crowds for Dodgers, Giants

The Giants left the Polo Grounds after the 1957
season because, according to owner Horace
Stoneham, the facility was old and outdated and
located in one of the city's high-crime areas. Nothing
had changed when the Mets entered the league
in 1962 and took over the stadium. Stoneham's
detractors referenced the Mets' ability to draw
922,530 fans to upper Manhattan in their first season
and 1,080,108 in their second as proof that the owner's claims were bogus.

However, the Mets ability to draw an average of
one million people to the Polo Grounds those first
two seasons probably had more to do with the fans'
allegiance to the two teams that bolted in 1958
than anything to do with the Mets themselves.
Of the 14 times that the Mets drew more than 20,000
to Coogan's Bluff in 1962, their opponent each time
was either the Dodgers or Giants. And of the 19 times
20,000 or more trekked to the Polo Grounds in 1963,
13 were with the Giants or Dodgers in the visitor's
dugout. When the team moved to Shea Stadium out in
Queens in 1964, they drew an average of 1.7 million
fans per year for the next five seasons even though
they never finished higher than ninth place.

Memorable Ending to a Forgettable Career

Joe Pignatano is remembered more for his 13-year tenure as a pitching coach with the Mets than for any impact he made during his brief six-year career (1957–62) as a backup catcher with the Dodgers, A's, Giants and Mets. The Brooklyn native was signed by the Dodgers right out of high school in 1948 but didn't make it to the big leagues until 1957. He moved with the Dodgers to Los Angeles and was a member of their 1959 championship team. By 1962, he was nearing the end of the road and was sold for cash to the Mets from San Francisco on July 13, 1962.

In the final game of the season against the Cubs at Wrigley Field on September 30, Pignatano came to the plate for what would be his last at-bat of his career. In the top of the eighth with no outs and teammates Sammy Drake on second and Richie Ashburn on first, the future bullpen coach hit a line drive right into the glove of second baseman Ken Hubbs, who threw it to first baseman Ernie Banks, who then fired the ball to shortstop Andre Rodgers to complete the triple play. One inning later, the game ended in a 5–1 Chicago win, and the Mets closed out the season with the worst record in baseball history, 40–120.

Eight years earlier in 1955, while he was a player in the Dodgers farm system, Pignatano figured prominently in another dubious incident. Playing for the Fort Worth Cats in a game on May 29 against the Shreveport Sports, the catcher was listed as the eighth batter in the lineup. In the second inning, he went to the plate in the seventh spot and hit a home run.

Shreveport appealed the play and the home run was nullified, and future Hall of Famer Maury Wills, the proper seventh batter, was called out. Next up, now in his proper position in the order, Pignatano returned to the batter's box and promptly hit another homer.

Milestones Frontwards and Backwards

There was very little for Mets fans to cheer about during the team's early years as the basement dwellers of the National League. Mets management resorted to signing or trading for aging stars who at least were once great: Duke Snyder, Gil Hodges and Yogi Berra. On June 14, 1963, Snyder hit a two-run homer off Bob Purkey of the Reds in Cincinnati for a 10–3 win. It was the former Dodgers star's 400th career home run, yet the career milestone was, for the most part, ignored by the local New York media. Outfielder Jimmy Piersall, who had recently joined the Mets, teased Snyder about the lack of recognition for reaching a mark that only six others had ever hit. Piersall, who had 99 career home runs at the time, boasted that he'd get more publicity for hitting his 100th than Snyder did for number 400.

Two weeks later, on June 26, Piersall hit home run number 100 off Dallas Green of the Phillies in a game at the Polo Grounds. As Piersall reached first and began to head for second base, he turned around and, with his back now facing second base, continued his home-run trot backwards the rest of the way. The hometown fans gave him a standing ovation, and his prediction came true as his home-run trot made headlines from coast-to-coast the next day.

Mets manager Casey Stengel, however, was not amused. Piersall, who had a reputation for absurd and at times irrational behavior, was released several days later.

Mr. Big Apple Baseball

You had to have a sense of humor to manage the Mets during their early years in the league. Perhaps that's why owner Joan Payson hired Charles Dillon "Casey" Stengel to guide the collection of old, former All-Stars and young players whom other teams felt weren't worth keeping. In choosing Stengel, who just two years earlier had been forcibly "retired" by the Yankees after they lost the 1960 World Series to the Pirates, Payson hoped to prove to New York's National League fan base that she was committed to building a winner. And despite the loss in 1960, Stengel had just finished a stint with the cross-town rival Yankees where he won 10 pennants and seven championships in 12 seasons, from 1949 to 1960. Stengel, whose malapropos rivaled even Yogi Berra's, provided good copy for the sports writers and helped divert fans' attention from a team that lost over 100 games in each of Stengel's four seasons as Mets manager.

After spending more than 50 years playing, coaching and managing in professional baseball, Stengel retired for good in 1965. One of his more insightful observations learned through his half century in the game proved helpful to future managers: "The secret of managing is to keep the guys who hate you away from the guys who are undecided."

His jokes, however, masked an excellent baseball mind steeped in a half-century's worth of experience in the game. Stengel, who was born in 1890 in Kansas City, Missouri, began his 14-year playing career in 1912 with the Dodgers. He starred on Brooklyn's 1916 pennant-winning squad and eventually played in two more World Series with the Giants against the Yankees in 1922 and 1923. He hit .300 three times and had the distinction of hitting the first-ever home run in Ebbets Field in 1913 and his inside-the-park home run against the Yankees in the 1923 series was the first World Series round-tripper hit in the Yankees' new park. In 12 post-season games, Stengel boasted an impressive .393 batting average. He enjoyed a good joke and didn't hesitate to use himself as a source for comedic material. "I broke in with four hits and the writers promptly declared they had seen the new Ty Cobb," he once recalled. "It took me only a few days to correct that impression."

Casey's playing days ended in 1925, and he went into coaching and managing, mostly at the minor league level. His first two managerial stints came with the Dodgers (1934–36) and the Boston Braves (1938–43), but neither team finished higher than fifth place. During World War II and in the years immediately after the war, Stengel enjoyed managerial success with minor league teams in Milwaukee and San Francisco. That's what caught the attention of the Yankees, who tabbed him as their new skipper in 1949.

At age 58, Stengel found it much easier filling out a lineup card that featured future Hall of Famers Joe DiMaggio, Yogi Berra, Phil Rizzuto, Whitey Ford and Mickey Mantle. Not every player in pinstripes was a baseball immortal, and Stengel began a platoon system that maximized the abilities of role players on the roster, which helped the Yankees win a record five consecutive World Series from 1949 to 1953. Legendary manager Connie Mack remarked, "I never saw a man who juggled his lineup so much and who played so many hunches so successfully." After finishing second in 1954, the Yanks won another four pennants and two championships from 1955 to 1958 before winning their 10th and final pennant under Stengel in 1960.

Stengel's success with the Yankees is the main reason why he was elected into the Hall of Fame in 1966. Judging from his lack of success with the Dodgers, Braves and Mets (he never finished higher than fifth), some questioned Stengel's managerial prowess. Hall of Fame pitcher Warren Spahn, who pitched for Stengel with the hapless Braves and Mets, quipped a line that would have brought a smile to the "Old Professor" himself, "I played for Casey before *and* after he was a genius."

No MVPs

The Mets have had their share of extraordinary players during their 60-year history. While Don Clendenon (1969) and Ray Knight (1986) both won the Babe Ruth Award as the Most Valuable Player of the World Series, no Mets player has ever garnered enough votes to win the National League MVP Award for a regular season. The best showing came from Tom Seaver, who finished second to San Francisco first baseman Willie McCovey in 1969. Yet several Mets players have won the award while playing for other teams: Willie Mays (San Francisco Giants, twice), George Foster (Cincinnati Reds), Kevin Mitchell (San Francisco Giants) and Ricky Henderson (Oakland A's).

Still No No-Nos

Every starting pitcher dreams of pitching a no-hitter or a perfect game, but for Mets pitchers, it still remains an unfulfilled dream. In the five decades since the team entered MLB, not a single Mets hurler has accomplished either feat. This is a distinction shared with just one other club, the San Diego Padres. Yet several quality hurlers who have worn a Mets uniform turned in pitching gems for teams after they left Flushing. Nolan Ryan tossed a record seven no-hitters in the 1970s and '80s for the Angels, Astros and Rangers. Tom Seaver came close during his 11 years in New York, tossing five one-hitters. One year and a day after he was traded to Cincinnati, the man once known as "The Franchise" held St. Louis hitless in a 4–0 win in June 1978.

Mike Scott, who nearly single-handedly kept the Mets out of the 1986 World Series, struck out 13 and walked two in Houston's 2–0 win over San Francisco on September 25, 1986. Dwight Gooden and David Cone both enjoyed 20-game winning seasons with the Mets, but it was as members of the hated Yankees that they had their career days. Gooden beat the Seattle Mariners 2–0 on May 14, 1996, at Yankee Stadium. Three years later, on a day when Don Larsen—the only pitcher to throw a perfect game in the World Series—tossed out the opening pitch, Cone was also flawless in a 6–0 win over the Montreal Expos. Hideo Nomo holds the distinction of pitching no-hitters before and after leaving the Mets.

The other nine hurlers who came to the Mets with no-hitters already on their resumés include Don Cardwell (Chicago Cubs), Warren Spahn (Milwaukee Braves), Dean Chance (Minnesota Twins), Dock Ellis (Pittsburgh Pirates), John Candelaria (Pittsburgh Pirates), Bret Saberhagen (Kansas City Royals), Al Leiter (Florida Marlins), Scott Erickson (Minnesota Twins) and Kenny Rogers (Texas Rangers). But to be fair, Mets pitchers have come close. On 35 occasions, Mets opponents have been held to just one hit. And on two occasions, Seaver took his no-hitter into the ninth inning.

Only One Hall of Famer

It's a bit shocking that in the 50-year history of the Mets, who have at times enjoyed moderate success, they have just one player enshrined in Cooperstown who spent the bulk of his productive years in New York. But the Mets did strike gold when they selected pitcher Tom Seaver in the first round of the 1966 amateur draft. "Tom Terrific" lived up to his promise by winning the National League Rookie of the Year honors in 1967, going 16–7 on a last-place team. The power-throwing right-hander had a winning record in all but one of the first 11 seasons in which he called Shea Stadium home.

Seaver still holds most of the team's pitching records. He struck out a then-record 19 batters in a game against San Diego in 1971. He threw five one-hitters as a Met, won three Cy Young Awards and led the National League in ERA (three times), strikeouts (five times) and wins (three times). He totaled at least 200 strikeouts a record 10 straight seasons. He finally closed his career in 1986 with a 311–205 record, with 3640 strikeouts and an ERA of 2.86 (the third lowest since 1920). He finally got his no-hitter, but it came as a Cincinnati Red in 1978. In a salute to the greatest player in their history, the Mets conferred the double honor on Seaver of throwing the last pitch at Shea Stadium in 2008 and the first pitch at the opening of Citi Field in 2009.

Joe Torre's Historic Game

The night of July 21, 1975, was a historic night for the Mets. New York second baseman Felix Millan went 4-for-4, all singles, against the Astros in Houston. Millan's four-hit night may have been noteworthy, but what followed was historic. Millan, hitting second in the lineup, was followed by veteran Joe Torre, who the Mets had acquired from the Cardinals in 1974. What made the night memorable was Torre grounding into four double plays, all at Millan's expense, thus setting a National League record and tying him with two players who had also turned the trick in the American League. When the future Yankees manager was told of his "record-setting" night, he quipped, "I couldn't have set a record without Millan. He ought to get an assist."

Hooray for Buckner!

To Red Sox fans, he is one of the most maligned players to ever don a Boston uniform, but to New York Mets fans, Bill Buckner is a hero. The Red Sox held a 3–2 edge over the Mets going into game six of the 1986 World Series when the teams took the field at Shea Stadium in Queens. The Red Sox hadn't been champions of baseball since 1918, while the Mets hadn't tasted the victor's champagne since their miracle year of 1969. Boston clung to a 3–2 lead going into the bottom of the eighth inning, but the Mets tied the score when Lee Mazzilli scored from third on Gary Carter's sacrifice fly. After a scoreless ninth inning, Boston pulled ahead 5–3 on Dave Henderson's solo home run and Marty Barrett's single that scored Wade Boggs. Boston was just three outs away from ending their 68-year drought.

Relief pitcher Calvin Schraldi retired the first two Mets batters, and the Red Sox were now on the top of the dugout steps ready to charge onto the field to begin their celebration. But then Carter singled. And Kevin Mitchell singled. Carter came around and scored on another single, this time Ray Knight's, cutting the deficit to 5–4. Schraldi was replaced by Bob Stanley to try to escape from New York with the win. The Mets' hopes now lay with Mookie Wilson, who stepped into the batter's box. But Stanley threw a wild pitch and Mitchell scored from third to tie the score at 5–5, and Ray Knight advanced to second. The fear of impending doom now lurked in the hearts of Red Sox fans. On the next pitch, Wilson hit a routine slow-roller toward

Buckner at first base, which should have ended the inning. But knowing Wilson was fast, Buckner tried to rush the play and allowed the ball to skip under his glove and into right field, allowing Knight to score the winning run from second base.

This is the play as called by CBS Radio's Jack Buck:

Here's the pitch to Mookie Wilson. Winning run at second. Ground ball to first; it is a run, an error! An error by Buckner! The winning run scores! The Mets win it six to five with three in the 10th! The ball went right through the legs of Buckner and the Mets with two men out and nobody on have scored three times to bring about a seventh game, which will be played here tomorrow night. Folks, it was unbelievable!...Well, open up the history book, folks; we've got an entry for you.

New York tortured Boston in game seven. The Red Sox took a 3–0 lead into the sixth inning, but the Mets rallied again and took the World Series with an 8–5 victory. Like their 1969 team, the 1986 edition of the Mets needed a few miracles to win the World Series. Buckner, who had an admirable 22-year career primarily with the Dodgers, Cubs and Red Sox, was cursed by Red Sox fans, but the Mets faithful could not thank him enough. The ball that squeaked by Buckner in game six is on display at the Mets Hall of Fame and Museum at Citi Field.

New York Yankees

The Bombers from The Bronx

When talking about baseball, or all sports for that matter in the Empire State and out across the fruited plain, the New York Yankees are the 500-pound gorilla in every conversation. The "Bronx Bombers" have won more championships and have featured players who personified their eras, like in the case of Babe Ruth, who remains the sport's biggest star and one of the greatest sports figures in history. But what the Yankees also symbolize is winning—they've not only won more World Series than the second, third and fourth winningest teams combined, but also their 27 world championships are equal to the combined total of every other professional sports team that calls, or once called, New York home.

The Origin of the Word "Yankee"

When Frank Ferrell and Bill Devery purchased a defunct Baltimore franchise from the American league and moved them to Manhattan in 1903, the original name for the team was the New York Highlanders. They were given this moniker because the site of the ballpark at 168th Street and Broadway was one of the highest spots on the island, therefore the name "Highlanders" seemed to apply. It wasn't until April 1913, when the Highlanders moved to the Polo Grounds, that they were officially renamed the Yankees. But what exactly is a "Yankee" anyway?

The origins of the word are uncertain, but it first turned up around the mid-1700s when British

General James Wolfe used the word to refer to the people of what was to become to the United States. He wrote the following in one of his communiqués, referring to Yankees in a somewhat derogatory manner: "My posts are now so fortified that I can afford you the two companies of Yankees, and the more as they are better for ranging and scouting than either work or vigilance."

Although it was the British that seemed to have coined the word, its origins actually lie with the Dutch. During the early 1700s in America, the Dutch and the early New Englanders often interacted and lived in the same neighborhoods. One theory for the origins of "Yankee" comes from the common Dutch names of "Jan" and "Kees"—the word "Jan-Kees" was then used to refer to those English settlers moving into the Dutch areas along the eastern coast. The term might have started as a slang term for the Dutch, but eventually it was extended to refer to the English colonists as well. Although it began as a derogatory term used by the snobby British to refer to the colonists, "Yankee" evolved into an affirmation and a source of pride during the American Revolutionary War (1775–83), as the lowly Yankees were able to fight off the British forces to create a new country of their own.

Because most Yankees were originally located along the northeast coast, the term was mostly associated with people living in that region. So when it came time for the New York Highlanders to choose a new name for their baseball team, history provided the perfect match for New York–based team, and the New York Yankees were born in 1913.

Future Famers Are Early Stars

The first two stars of the Highlanders were future Hall of Famers Willie Keeler and Jack Chesbro. Keeler, a Brooklynite, played for the Giants, Dodgers and Highlanders in a long career that spanned 19 seasons, from 1892 to 1910. He was regarded as one of the best hitters in the game, leading the National League in batting in 1897 and 1898 with .424 and .385, respectively. In 1904, the Highlanders' second season, pitcher Jack Chesbro led the American League in wins (41–12), ERA (1.82) and innings pitched (454). The workhorse started 51 of the 58 games he appeared in and accounted for a full third of the innings thrown that year by the nine-man staff.

They'd Get to See a Lot More of Those

The 1915 season was another unremarkable one for the Yankees. They got off to a good start and were in second place when the Red Sox came to town on May 6 to open a three-game series. They beat Boston in the series opener 4–3 in a 13-inning affair, but the 8000 fans on hand at the Polo Grounds that day witnessed a historical moment—although no one knew it at the time. Boston's 20-year-old starting pitcher went the distance and picked up the loss. But in the third inning, Yankee pitcher Jack Warhop was victimized by his Red Sox counterpart, who, batting left-handed, drove the ball into the upper deck of the right-field grandstands for his first career home run.

Legendary sportswriter Damon Runyon, who covered the game, wrote of the young second-year player who would eventually become the best left-handed pitcher in the American League, "He is now quite the demon pitcher and hitter when he connects." You might recognize the pitcher's name; it was Babe Ruth.

Hall of Fame Ability, Major League Headache

Most historians of the pre-1920s consider Ray Caldwell one of the top talents in the game. Unfortunately, his lack of character and penchant for self-indulgence eventually outweighed his potential, which he never fulfilled. Like Boston's emerging young star Babe Ruth, the right-handed pitcher who batted left was considered a double threat; he occasionally played the outfield and was also used as a pinch hitter.

Caldwell's best season on the mound for the Yankees was 1914, when he went 18–9 with a 1.94 ERA. Several seasons were marred by injuries, but off the field, he was a heavy drinker and made himself a consistent disciplinary problem for management. He was fined and suspended several times during his nine years in New York (1910–18) and was once charged with grand larceny and failure to provide child support.

What caused the Yankees' frustrations was Caldwell's indifference to the havoc he caused others and himself. It was those rare occasions when Caldwell was sober and healthy and showed what he was capable of that prompted management to give him numerous chances. One of those games occurred on July 10, 1917, when he tossed 9⅔ innings without allowing a hit as a reliever in a 7–5 win over the St. Louis Browns.

Caldwell was traded to Boston after the 1918 season, but he was not through with tormenting the Yankees. The pitcher wore out his welcome in Boston and was released in August 1919 then was immediately signed by Cleveland. He returned to New York on September 10 to face his old teammates. In the opening game of a doubleheader at the Polo Grounds, Caldwell went the distance without allowing a hit as the Indians beat the Yankees 3–0. He went 20–10 for the Indians in 1920, but again wore out his welcome the following season, which was his last. Hall of Fame managers Miller Huggins and Connie Mack both thought Caldwell possessed Hall of Fame–level talent. As it was, his career ended at age 33, with a mediocre 134–120 record over 12 seasons.

Death on the Diamond

Carl Mays was one of the best pitchers of his era and was also one of the key players the Yankees acquired from the Red Sox that laid the foundation for their first of many pennant-winning teams. The right-hander with a submarine motion was the mainstay of the staff, going 26–10 in 1920 and 27–9 in 1921. Mays was one of the more successful applicants of the spitball, which was legal at the time, and also scuffed the ball up, causing it to make unusual movements as it traveled from the mound to home plate. He did not like hitters crowding the plate and would often throw high and inside to brush them back, which resulted in batters bailing out, hitting the deck or getting hit by the pitch. Although successful in Boston and New York, Mays was not well liked by his Yankee teammates, and because of his reputation as a headhunter, he was one of the most unpopular players of his era as well.

It was those two components of Mays' pitching repertoire that proved fatal to Cleveland shortstop Ray Chapman. The Indians and Yankees, neither of whom had ever finished in first place, were locked in a tight pennant race when the Tribe came to the Polo Grounds on August 16, 1920. Cleveland, at 70–40, held a half-game lead over the Yankees, who were sending their ace, Mays, to the mound to open the three-game series. Chapman was in the ninth year of his career and had developed into a solid ballplayer; he had hit over .300 in three of his last four seasons.

In the top of the fifth inning, Chapman stepped in against Mays with the Indians ahead 4–0. By all accounts, Chapman either didn't see the pitch or froze as the fastball Mays threw struck the Indian shortstop directly in the head. The sound of the ball hitting Chapman's skull and the distance it traveled back to the mound confused Mays, who thought the ball had actually hit Chapman's bat. The pitcher fielded the ground ball between the mound and first base and threw to first baseman Wally Pipp.

Chapman collapsed with blood coming from his left ear. The umpire immediately approached the stands asking for any doctors to come forward. Yankee catcher Muddy Ruel tried to grab the Indian shortstop as he fell. After being administered by two doctors, Chapman was helped to his feet and escorted by teammates toward the clubhouse, which was located in centerfield. But Chapman collapsed again near second base and had to be carried off the field. He was rushed to a nearby hospital and underwent surgery in an attempt to save his life, but he died early the next morning.

Chapman's wife, Kathleen, left Cleveland for New York as soon as she was notified of the accident, but her husband of less than two years died before she got there. Players on other American League teams, many of whom already disliked Mays, called for his banishment, foremost among them Ty Cobb of the Detroit Tigers. The Indians–Yankees game of August 17 was canceled as Chapman's teammates and a few Yankees escorted the player's remains back to Cleveland. Yankee manager Miller Huggins left Mays in New York on the Yankees next road trip to Cleveland, which went on to win its first pennant despite the loss of Chapman, and then defeated Brooklyn in the World Series.

The spitball, which was being phased out of baseball at the time, was banned altogether following the 1920 season. Mays pitched for the Yankees through the 1923 season and then was sold to Cincinnati, where he went 20–9 in 1924. He pitched for the Reds through

1928 and retired following a 7–2 campaign with the Giants in 1929. Despite a 208–126 career record, which included five 20-game winning seasons, Mays is not in the Hall of Fame. Unfortunately, Chapman's death was the first in a series of tragedies for his wife, who was pregnant with the couple's first child when her husband died. She gave birth to a girl, Rae, and eventually remarried and moved to California. But she later suffered a nervous breakdown and died after drinking a poisonous liquid in 1926. Three years later, Rae died during a measles epidemic.

Baseball Crowns New Home Run King

Midway through his second season with the Yankees, Babe Ruth entered the record books as the all-time home run king. On July 18, 1921, Babe belted his 36th home run of the season and 139th of his career as he passed Roger Connor, who spent 10 of his 18 seasons (1880–97) with the New York Giants. Ruth, who was all of 26 at the time, retired during the 1935 season with an astonishing 714 home runs. He led the American League in that department a record 12 times and all of baseball 11 times. When he left the game, only one other player, Lou Gehrig, had passed the 300 mark. Ruth's career total held up until Hank Aaron passed him in 1974. It took Aaron, who finished with 755 round trippers, 11,295 at-bats to hit number 715; the Babe needed only 8399. Unlike a certain convicted felon who played for the San Francisco Giants from 1993 to 2007 and is given credit by Major League Baseball for hitting 762 home runs, neither Ruth nor Aaron used performance-enhancing drugs.

The Babe Christens New Home

When Yankee Stadium opened in 1923, it was a state-of-the-art facility and the first triple-decked stadium in the world. Opening day was a grand event as a crowd of approximately 75,000 jammed "The House That Ruth Built," with as much as 25,000 hopefuls turned away. The U.S. Marine Corps Band, under the direction of none other than John Phillip Sousa, provided the pregame entertainment. Once the game started, the two-time defending American League champions beat the Red Sox 4–1 behind the pitching of staff ace Bob Shawkey. It was the Babe himself who christened the ballpark with a fourth-inning solo homer. Ruth achieved another, more dubious distinction that day—"The Bambino" dropped a fly ball in the fifth inning and also became the first Yankee to commit an error in their new home.

Shocking End to 1926 World Series

No player has set more records and left more fans and opponents numb from his dominance than Babe Ruth. Yet one time, he left his opponents baffled and his teammates disappointed. It came during the ninth inning of game seven of the 1926 World Series against the Cardinals. Ruth had enjoyed a solid performance in that year's Fall Classic, going 6-for-20. And in game four, he became the first player in World Series history to smack three home runs in a single game.

His solo homer in the fourth inning of game seven accounted for one of the Yankee runs in a game they trailed 3–2 entering the bottom of the ninth inning.

With two outs, the Babe walked for a record 11th time. Next up was cleanup hitter Bob Meusel, who faced pitcher Grover Cleveland Alexander. The Yankee leftfielder, who was a career .309 hitter and batted .315 in 1926, had had a double and triple off the future Hall of Fame pitcher in game six. With the count 0-and-1, Meusel awaited Alexander's second pitch. Ruth, who had always been regarded as a good yet overly aggressive base runner during his career, suddenly took off for second base. Meusel swung and missed, and Cardinals catcher Bob O'Farrell fired the ball to second baseman Rogers Hornsby, who waited and easily tagged Ruth out—it wasn't even close—to give St. Louis the championship.

Toward the end of his career, Ruth asked team ownership for a chance to manage the Yankees. The conventional wisdom is that the owners thought, given the Babe's rowdy behavior as a younger player, how could he manage two dozen men when he couldn't manage himself? Or perhaps they remembered the abrupt ending to the 1926 World Series. With that decisive game on the line, just one, and only one, man thought it was a good idea to have Ruth try to steal second base, and that was Babe himself.

Murderer's Row: None Better

Just how good were the 1927 Yankees? Led by Babe Ruth and Lou Gehrig, the best one-two punch in history, they went 110–42. They finished 19 games ahead of second-place Philadelphia, and then swept Pittsburgh 4–0 in the World Series. Their .714 winning percentage was tied for second best of the 20th century. The 1906 Cubs won 116 games but lost the World Series to the White Sox. The 1909 Pirates' 110–42 equaled the Yanks, and they won the World Series over Detroit, but Honus Wagner was the only offense "threat" in their lineup. The future Hall of Fame shortstop was the only Pirates player to hit over .300 and drive in 100 runs.

The '27 Yankees earned the nickname "Murderer's Row" and, at the same time, lived up to their growing reputation as the "Bronx Bombers." Five of the eight everyday players hit over .300: Gehrig (.373), Ruth (.356), Tony Lazzeri (.309), Bob Meusel (.337) and leadoff hitter Earl Combs (.356). Ruth hit 60 home runs and had 164 RBI; he was followed by Gehrig (47, 175), Lazzeri (18, 102) and Meusel (8, 103).

As a team, the Yankees led the majors in hitting (.307), home runs, runs scored and doubles and triples. Individually, Ruth led the majors in homers, walks, on-base percentage and slugging percentage, but finished second to Gehrig—the man who followed him in the batting order—in total bases, extra base hits and RBI. Gehrig was tops in RBI, doubles, extra base hits and total bases, but finished second to the Bambino in homers, on-base percentage, slugging percentage and walks. Combs was tops in at-bats, plate appearances and edged Gehrig in triples, but finished second to Pittsburgh's Paul Waner in hits. Led by future Hall of Famer Waite Hoyt, who led Yankee starters with a 22–7 record, the team also finished ahead of the other 15 teams in baseball—and not just the American League—in every major team pitching category. Although not as dominating in 1928, the same contingent repeated as world champions.

"Now Batting, Number 3—Babe Ruth!"

Around 1915, teams began to experiment with numbers on the sleeves of players' jerseys in order to help fans identify their favorite players but in the increasingly larger stadiums, the tiny number made little difference. In 1929, the Yankees again saw their team beginning to attract many new fans, who were unfamiliar with the players by appearance. In order to help new fans get acquainted with the Yankees, the team put large numbers on the back of each player's jersey. In the beginning, these numbers were handed out not on the basis of player preference for a certain number but in the order in which they batted; for example, Babe Ruth batted third, therefore he received the number 3. Later, numbers were assigned at random or by special request.

A Babe Smokes Babe

It was the spring of 1931, and Joe Engel, owner of the Southern Association's AA Chattanooga Lookouts, was looking for a way to bring more people out to see his team. Engel soon got wind of a talented, unsigned female pitcher with a killer sinker that would fit perfectly into his lineup and provide a little sensationalism at the same time. Engel signed 17-year-old Jackie Mitchell to a contract and hoped that she would provide the "edge" he needed to get fans into the grandstands.

All of Chattanooga was buzzing with excitement because Mitchell was billed as the first and only female to start a pitching assignment for an all-male team. (In reality, Lizzy Arlington had already broken the gender barrier in 1898 when she pitched one game for a Reading, Pennsylvania, team against a neighboring team from Allentown.) After impressing her teammates in practice, Mitchell got to show off her skills during an exhibition game when the New York Yankees rolled into town.

It was customary during those days that a team like the Yankees travel the back roads of the country and play in exhibition games against their farm teams. In April 1931, the Yankees rolled into town with much fanfare, and 4000 fans packed in at the local field along with a throng of media to get a glimpse of the Yankees famed "Murderer's Row."

The Chattanooga Lookouts started the game with pitcher Bert Niehoff on the mound, but after surrendering a double and a single, the manager called out for a replacement. The Yankees bench looked on in shock as Jackie Mitchell stepped onto the diamond and took up her position on the mound. As if the pressure of being a woman in a man's league wasn't enough for the young pitcher, Mitchell's first batter was the "Sultan of Swat" himself, Babe Ruth.

Ruth walked up to the mound with a huge grin on his face, ready to teach the young woman a big-league lesson. Ruth calmly allowed the first pitch, a sinker, to sail by for a ball. The Bambino then swung at the next two sinkers and missed for two strikes, causing Ruth to grumble angrily to himself. Realizing that Mitchell's pitching arsenal consisted of basically just a sinker and a fastball, Ruth decided to watch the next pitch sail by, knowing that she would try to get him to fish for a third strike. Her fourth pitch just caught the corner of the strike zone, and the umpire called the Bambino out. Embarrassed, Ruth stomped back to the dugout to lick his wounds.

Next batter up was the great Lou "Iron Horse" Gehrig. But he did no better than his teammate, striking out on three straight pitches. The crowd could hardly believe their eyes. With just seven pitches, Mitchell had sat down two of the greatest players in the history of baseball. Tony Lazzeri was up next, and he performed much better than his team-mates, drawing four straight balls for the walk. After letting Lazzeri reach first, Mitchell's moment in the spotlight was suddenly over. Without explanation, she was pulled from the game, but not before facing three of the greatest Yankees, striking out two and walking one. Despite her heroics, the Yankees went on to win the game 14–4.

A few days later, league commissioner Kenesaw Mountain Landis officially cut off Mitchell's career path to the big leagues by voiding her contract. His reasoning was that baseball was "too strenuous" for a woman. More likely he did not want to have her bruise the egos of any more of his male ball players. If she could strike out Babe Ruth, what would she do to the lesser players? But Landis could not stop Mitchell from going down in the history books as the teenage girl who struck out two of the greatest baseball players in the history of the game.

The Called Shot

It is one of those moments in the history of baseball that is more legend than fact. Even if you are not the biggest baseball fan, odds are that you know of the time that Babe Ruth stepped up to the plate during the third game of the 1932 World Series, pointed to the centerfield bleachers and cracked a home run exactly where he had pointed.

The 1932 World Series pitted the Cubs (90–64) against the Yankees (107–47). The Yankees took a 2–0 lead in the Fall Classic as the teams headed to Wrigley Field for game three. With superior pitching and a lineup of players that included Babe Ruth, Lou Gehrig and Tony Lazzeri, the Yankees were considered public enemy number one of the Chicago fans, particularly Ruth, who was the main target of hecklers. The taunting increased after Babe smacked a two-run home run early in the game. And the crowd let Ruth have an earful when he made an error in left field that led to a Cubs run and tied the score. Ever the showman, Ruth tipped his hat to the crowd. He loved the attention and decided to have a little more fun with the crowd the next time he stepped up to the plate.

Cubs starting pitcher Charley Root was on the mound and certainly didn't want to surrender another home run when Ruth stepped to the plate in the fifth inning. With every thrown strike, a chorus of cheers erupted from the crowd, and with each strike, Ruth extended one finger, and then two, to indicate to the crowd that he was well aware of the count. With the count at three balls and two strikes, he paused in the batter's box and pointed his bat toward the centerfield bleachers, as if he was signaling a home run.

Root wound up for the pitch and whipped the ball down the very center of the strike zone. Ruth swung with all his might and sent the ball to the very same spot to which he had pointed just moments earlier. As Ruth rounded the bases, he taunted the fans as well as the Cubs on the field and in the dugout. What's seldom mentioned is that the next hitter, Gehrig, torched Root for his second home run as the Yankees won 7–5. They completed the sweep the next day with a 13–6 drubbing.

Legend says that he was pointing to where he would hit his home run, but a home movie of the play in question that surfaced years later appears to show Ruth pointing to the number of strikes on the scoreboard in order to further taunt the Cubs bench.

No major newspaper account the next day mentioned a "called shot," and Ruth himself admitted a few times that he had not called the home run, but after the story got around, he never seemed to deny it. Charley Root denied that Ruth ever signaled the home run until the day he died. Even though it's unlikely that Ruth called the home run, the story has grown beyond truth and has become pure legend.

Out of Babe's Shadow, But...

By 1934, Babe Ruth's skills had faded, and the star of the team was now Lou Gehrig, who for the first time in his career bested Babe in home runs, RBI and batting average in the same season. Not only was Gehrig the statistical leader of the Yanks, but he also finished ahead of every American Leaguer in those three categories to win the Triple Crown. However, when it came to determining the league's Most Valuable Player, the sports writers awarded catcher Mickey Cochrane of the pennant-winning Tigers with the honor.

Gehrig wasn't second, third or fourth, either. Even thought the Iron Horse led the Yankees to a second-place finish with 49 homers, 165 RBI and batted .363, he only finished fifth in MVP voting. Upon closer examination, this isn't as shocking as it seems. A year earlier, Chuck Klein of the Phillies won the Triple, but Giants pitcher Carl Hubbell won the National League MVP. And Ted Williams, who holds the distinction of being the only player to win two Triple Crowns (1942, 1947), won his two American League MVP Awards in 1946 and 1949, respectively.

The Iron Horse vs. The Rock

After Gehrig retired from the Yankees, New York City mayor Fiorello LaGuardia appointed Lou as a parole commissioner in the hope that meeting the Yankee slugger, who took his new job seriously, would inspire troubled youths to straighten out their lives. When 19-year-old Thomas Rocco Barbella came before Gehrig for parole violation in 1940, the former Yankee great walked into the hearing room on crutches. "Every time he makes a step, I could see all the pain on the guy's face and it's hurting me worse than him," Barbella recalled years later. Gehrig lectured the young, Brooklyn native and said that, based on the parole violation and his prior criminal history, Barbella would be going back to Riker's Island.

Although furious with Gehrig's decision at the time, Barbella spent the rest of his time in jail turning his life around. "[Gehrig] probably saved my life," he said. The former teen hood channeled his energy into boxing and turned professional when he left prison. He eventually won the middleweight championship of the world and became one of the most beloved sports heroes in the city's history. But he did it under an assumed name, Rocky Graziano.

Luckiest Kid on the Face of the Earth

Pete Sheehy is a name known to most Yankee fans, but it's not one you'll find in any baseball record book or on old highlight reels. He didn't make any trades in the front office, coach players or win a single game as manager. Yet Sheehy's career with the Yankees lasted longer than any player, coach, manager or owner. His 58 years with the organization is one longer than Bob Sheppard, who performed his duties as Yankee Stadium announcer from 1951 to 2007. While waiting outside the stadium watching the players enter before a home game in 1927, Sheehy was spotted by clubhouse manager Fred Logan who needed help and asked the 15-year-old, "Hey kid, you want to come inside and give me a hand?"

Sheehy, who never played baseball, didn't hesitate and walked through the door and began working for the only organization he'd ever draw a regular paycheck from, eventually becoming the clubhouse manager. With the exception of his military service in World War II, Sheehy remained in that role until his death in 1985 at age 73. He was on hand for all the great moments, from Babe's single season, record-setting 60th home run in 1927, to Lou Gehrig's farewell, Joe DiMaggio's 56-game hitting streak, Don Larsen's perfect game and Roger Maris' 61st homer. Sheehy got to know the legendary players on a first-name basis and was well respected throughout the organization. Manager Casey Stengel once said of Sheehy, "That man is the most important worker [owners] Dan Topping and Del Webb have in the organization. He sees and hears everything, says nothing, and works twice as hard as anybody else."

Joe D Streaks to Record Book

By 1941, Joe DiMaggio was the biggest star on baseball's best team. He entered the season as the two-time defending batting champion and had averaged

34 homers and 138 RBI in his five seasons since joining the Yankees as a 21-year-old rookie in 1936. On May 15, he singled in the first inning of a 13–1 loss to the White Sox before an announced crowd of 9040 in a Thursday afternoon game at Yankee Stadium. DiMaggio and the Yankees had gotten off to a slow start that season; he entered the game hitting just .306. The loss left the Yankees in fourth place with a record of 14–15, 6.5 games behind the first-place Indians.

Including the game on May 15 against Chicago, DiMaggio got at least one hit in a record 56 consecutive games. DiMaggio's hitting streak captivated the nation in the summer of 1941 and was a welcome diversion from the war news from Europe. "Joltin' Joe" went 91-for-223 (.408) with 15 home runs and 55 RBI until he was held hitless in three trips to the plate (including a walk) on July 17 against the Indians in Cleveland. The Yanks went 41–13–2 during the streak and surged to first place, seven games ahead of the Indians. To put DiMaggio's feat in perspective, consider that no player since 1900 has even gotten a hit in 55 of 56 games. And DiMaggio's 61-game hitting streak in 1933 with the San Francisco Seals of the Pacific Coast League is the second longest in minor league history.

Joe D's 1941 MVP Season Continues

Joe DiMaggio wasn't one to rest on his laurels, regardless how great they were. When asked one time why he always tried so hard, DiMaggio replied, "I always played as if there was at least one person in the stands who had never seen me play." A day after

Cleveland held him hitless, the Yankee centerfielder went 2-for-4 and hit safely in his next 16 games. That's 72 out of 73. During the second streak, he went 29-for-68 (.426) with five home runs and 20 RBI. From May 15 to August 2, the "Yankee Clipper" hit an astounding .412 with 20 home runs and 75 RBI. On May 15, he was hitting .306; by August 2, his average had climbed to .381.

While their centerfielder cooled off, the Yankees finished strong. They won 30 of their last 35 games and took the pennant by 17 games and then beat the Dodgers in the World Series. Before the season ended, DiMaggio's teammates acknowledged that his hot bat in May, June and July had turned the season around. On August 29, the team threw a private dinner and presented DiMaggio with a sterling silver humidor. On the cover was a statuette of the eventual American League Most Valuable Player in his classic swing. On one side was "56" for the streak; on the other was "91" for the number of hits during the streak. The inscription read: "Presented to Joe DiMaggio by his fellow players on the New York Yankees to express their admiration for his consecutive-game hitting record, 1941." Below that, there were the engraved autographs of all his teammates.

Yogi Hangs on, for History

Although he's not in the Hall of Fame, Allie Reynolds ranks near the top of great Yankee pitchers. Called "The Chief" because of his Native American heritage, Reynolds had a winning record for all nine of his seasons in pinstripes (1946–54). His highest win total came in 1952, when he went 20–7 and led the American League in ERA (2.06). But 1951 was even more memorable for The Chief. On July 12 in Cleveland, he out-dueled Indian great Bob Feller 1–0 without allowing a hit. It was the first no-hitter thrown by a Yankees pitcher since Monte Pearson in 1928.

The Yankees and Reynolds would only have to wait until September 28 for the next no-hitter. Against the Red Sox on the last weekend of the season, Reynolds struck out nine and walked four and just needed one more out in the ninth inning. All that stood between him and his second gem of the season was Ted Williams. "The Splendid Splinter" popped a pitch in foul territory near the Yankee dugout. Catcher Yogi Berra ran under the ball, and with the fans on their feet cheering, Berra dropped the ball. It's sheer folly to give a hitter of Williams' stature a second chance. But on this day, the baseball gods were with Reynolds and Berra as Williams popped up the next pitch into almost the exact same place. This time, Berra made the play, and Reynolds became only the second pitcher in history to throw two no-hitters in the same season.

Mick Passes Babe Ruth

Mickey Mantle entered the 1964 World Series against the Cardinals with 15 career home runs in the Fall Classic, which tied him with Babe Ruth for the all-time lead. With the score tied 1–1 in the bottom of the ninth of game three, Mantle stepped in against St. Louis reliever Barney Shultz.

Batting left-handed against the 37-year-old Cardinal, Mantle drove the first pitch deep into the right field stands to give the Yanks a 2–1 win, and in doing so, he passed the Bambino. Mantle belted two more home runs and finished his career with 18 in World Series play, a record that still stands.

One Day Later: From Hero to "Groat"

Mickey Mantle provided Yankee fans with many memorable moments. His then-career record 1710 career strikeouts is one "record" he'd have preferred to have done without. But perhaps Mantle's most embarrassing moment in his 18-year career came in the bottom of the third inning of game four of the 1964 World Series against the Cardinals. With two outs and nobody on and the Yankees leading 3–0, Mantle was walked by pitcher Roger Craig then moved to second when Elston Howard also earned a base on balls.

At that moment, St. Louis shortstop Dick Groat went to speak to pitcher Craig. The two huddled and talked strategy. When Groat returned to his position, Mantle stepped off second. Groat slowly moved behind Mantle. Unbeknownst to "The Mick," his Yankee teammates and the 66,312 fans gathered at Yankee Stadium, Craig had slipped Groat the ball during their little pow-wow. As an unsuspecting Mantle took his lead off second base, Groat tagged him out to end the inning. Mantle had just become a victim of the "hidden ball" trick. It had been employed on unsuspecting base runners since the

1920s and may work about once a year, but in the World Series, and on national television? Ouch!

The Yanks only had one hit the rest of the game, and St. Louis rallied with a Ken Boyer grand slam in the eighth inning for a 4–3 win to tie the series at two games apiece. The Yanks went on to lose to the Cards four games to three in what would be their last appearance in the Fall Classic for 12 years.

Michael the Magician

Gene Michael joined the Yankees in 1968 and was their starting shortstop until 1974. Michael was never an All-Star, but he became a "master," if you will, of the "hidden ball" trick. The 6-foot-4 Michael, who was known as "The Stick," successfully pulled off the caper five times during his playing career in New York. When his playing days ended, Michael coached and managed the Yankees and the Cubs before becoming the Yankees general manager in the early 1990s. With some of the patience and shrewdness that allowed him to hoodwink unsuspecting base runners during his career, Michael acquired many of the players who became the foundation for the championship teams of the late-'90s, including Derek Jeter, Mariano Rivera, Andy Pettitte, Jorge Posada and Paul O'Neill.

Looks Can Be Deceiving

The nine-year period that CBS owned the Yankees (1964–72) was a time that their fans came to consider as the "dark ages" of the franchise. There were a few good players coming up through the farm system, but none was considered Hall of Fame talent. This was still the pre–free agent era, when fans were at the mercy of the front office to make trades and build a talented farm system. The 1970 Yankees featured budding talent in outfielders Roy White and Bobby Murcer, and rookie catcher Thurman Munson. On the mound, Mel Stottelmeyer, Fritz Peterson and reliever Lindy McDaniel powered the Yanks to a surprising 93–69 second-place finish, their best since 1964.

But the team never seriously challenged the eventual World Series champion Orioles, who were in the middle of three-straight American League pennant-winning seasons. Perhaps the most memorable day of the 1970 season occurred on the afternoon of June 24. School had just ended for the summer, so an unusually large crowd (for the time) of 30,000 was on hand for a Wednesday afternoon doubleheader at Yankee Stadium against the Indians. The Yankees dropped the opener 7–2, but they took the nightcap 5–4.

It was a career day for Murcer, who hit the first of four consecutive homers in the ninth inning of the first game and accounted for all five runs as he blasted three more homers in the nightcap. Some of the "entertainment" that afternoon took the form of "extracurricular" activities. A fight broke out between New York pitcher Stan Bahnsen and Cleveland's Vada Pinson, which prompted both dugouts to empty and culminated in a full-team brawl. Later on, a local miscreant lobbed a "Jerry bomb" firecracker, which exploded near Indians catcher Ray Fosse.

But the incident that made the highlight reel that day (and can still be viewed on YouTube) occurred in the ninth inning of the opener when Yankee reliever Steve Hamilton faced Cleveland slugger Tony Horton. Six-foot-six Hamilton was a solid reliever who had been with the Yankees since 1963. Prior to becoming a baseball player, Hamilton had played two seasons in the NBA for the Lakers. Late in his career, Hamilton developed and perfected a pitch he called the "Folly Floater," in which he slowed his delivery and then lobbed the ball high into the air to the unsuspecting batter. It was similar to the "Eephus Pitch" that Pittsburgh Pirates pitcher Rip Sewell threw to Ted Williams in the 1946 All-Star game.

Before the Midsummer Classic that year, Sewell told Williams that if they faced each other, the future Hall of Famer could expect to see his famous pitch. As promised, the "Splendid Splinter" fouled off two pitches before finally belting an Eephus for a home run. It was the only time Sewell had ever surrendered a home run with his famous pitch.

So, with the Yankees trailing 7–1, manager Ralph Houk gave the southpaw permission to throw the Folly Floater, which Horton, a decent power hitter, fouled into the stands behind the visiting dugout. The crowd began cheering for Hamilton to throw the pitch again, and Horton beckoned that he wanted another chance to smash the enticing looking "floater" for a home run. Hamilton threw the pitch again, and Horton fouled it high behind home plate, but this time it was run down and caught for an out by Munson.

With both teams and the crowd laughing, Horton threw up his hands with a "Hey, what can you do?" gesture and then dropped to his knees and crawled into the dugout. For all who witnessed the bizarre antics that afternoon, it was one of the more memorable days of an otherwise forgettable era.

The Mick's Last Hurrah

Mickey Mantle hit 536 home runs in the regular season and added 18 more in the World Series and two in All-Star games. However, one of the most memorable home runs he ever hit came five years after he retired. In August 1973, Mantle stepped to the plate in an exhibition game as part of the Yankees annual Old-Timers' Day festivities. The 1973 season would be the last in the old ballpark before the team temporarily moved to Shea Stadium for two seasons while Yankee Stadium was renovated. Batting right-handed against his good friend and old teammate Whitey Ford, Mantle fouled off a few pitches before Mel Allen, the master of ceremonies for the event, beckoned him over the public address system to "Straighten one out, Mick!" On Ford's next pitch, Mantle smacked one of his trademark high, arching blasts into the left-field stands and circled the bases to a standing ovation.

The Boomer Becomes First DH

Prior to 1973, American League pitchers, like their counterparts on the senior circuit, stepped into the batter's box in every game. In an attempt to add more scoring and excitement to the game, the American

League owners decided to replace the pitcher, who was usually an automatic out, with a regular, everyday-type player, or, as we know it now, a "designated hitter." On opening day in 1973, baseball trivia buffs anxiously waited to see which designated hitter would step into the batter's box for the historic first at bat. That distinction fell to Yankee Ron Blomberg.

The left-handed hitter, batting sixth in the lineup, walked in the top of the first against Luis Tiant. He later singled and finished the day 1-for-3. Blomberg, a first-round draft pick in 1967, came up briefly in 1969 before spending parts of six injury-plagued seasons with the Yankees. "The Boomer," as he was called, finally left New York with a career batting average of .302 in 400 games. He signed with the White Sox in 1978, but the injury plague followed him to the Windy City. After playing just 61 games, he retired from baseball at age 29.

The D&D Boys

That would be Dent and Doyle. By late July 1978, the Yankees trailed the Boston Red Sox by 14 games. Only the truest of believers held out hope that the Bronx Bombers would repeat as World Series champions. And if you told those loyalists that the hitting stars of the World Series were going to be shortstop Bucky Dent and utility infielder Brian Doyle, you would've been greeted with a "Bronx Cheer"—that endearing act in which one sticks their tongue partly out of their mouth and blows hard; it's not something you'll find in a Miss Manners manual.

But the unthinkable did happen. Doyle, who got to play in the post-season because starting second baseman Willie Randolph was injured, batted eighth in a lineup that featured Thurman Munson and Reggie Jackson. Doyle went 7-for-16 (.425), while Dent, hitting in his customary ninth position, went 10-for-24 (.417) and was voted MVP of the World Series as the Yankees beat the Dodgers for the second straight year.

Thanks, Kid!

Passionate baseball fan and New York Yankees devotee Jeffrey Maier had no idea he was about to make the history books as he walked into Yankee Stadium on October 9, 1996, as the Yankees took on the Baltimore Orioles in game one of the American League Championship. But late in the game, 12-year-old Jeffrey's desire to retrieve a souvenir changed not only the outcome of the game, and possibly the American League Championship, but arguably also the World Series.

Heading into the bottom of the eighth inning, the Orioles were holding on to a slim 4–3 advantage. The Yankees fans felt game one slowly slipping through their fingers. But the Yankees had Derek Jeter, and he was not about to give up on the game just yet. The shortstop stepped up to bat and connected with a hard fastball that made its way to the outfield fence. The ball appeared to have enough power behind it to make it over the fence, but Orioles outfielder Tony Tarasco knew he had a shot if he timed his catch just right. At that same moment, our young Yankee fan, Jeffrey, was sitting by the edge of the outfield fence and thought he could make the catch as well and score himself a nice souvenir. Tarasco and Jeffrey's gloves extended for the ball at the same time, but it was Maier who touched the ball first, though instead of catching it, the ball disappeared behind the fence.

"It was a magic trick because the ball just disappeared out of midair," said Tarasco after the game.

Immediately, the Orioles bench called for fan interference, but umpire Rich Garcia ruled that Jeter be awarded a home run. On the countless replays that followed, it could be clearly seen that Maier had interfered with the play, and league rules clearly state that if a fan prevents a player from catching the ball then the umpire has to call the batter out. The Orioles were so insistent that the wrong call was made that a complaint was filed with the Commissioner of Major League Baseball, Bud Selig, following the game. After considering the options, Selig ruled that the home run be upheld, and the series continued.

With the score tied, the game went into extra innings, and the Yankees won the game with an 11th-inning home run from Bernie Williams that easily cleared the fence. The Yankees went on to win the American League Championship four games to one and defeated the Atlanta Braves to win the World Series. In Baltimore, the local fans and media vilified young Jeffrey Maier for his interference, but in his hometown, the kid was treated as if he had hit a home run himself.

The Boss Places Third

In the wake of George Steinbrenner's death, the man who became known as "The Boss" received generally positive reviews for his stewardship of the team during his ownership from 1973 until his death in July 2010. Two months after Steinbrenner's death, a large plaque acknowledging his tenure and accomplishments was dedicated in the Monument Park at the new Yankee Stadium, which opened in 2009. The oversized shrine, which some baseball historians have deemed inappropriate, dwarfs that of all the Yankees' other great players and owners. While Steinbrenner certainly revived the franchise, he also was responsible for its darkest stretch since the era before Ruth joined the team.

It was owner Jacob Ruppert who first turned the Yankees into champions and built Yankee Stadium. Ruppert was a New York native and former congressman who served four terms (1899–1907). He bought the Yankees with partner Tillinghast L'Hommedieu Huston on December 31, 1915. At the time, the Yankees had never won a pennant and only finished as high as second, twice. Ruppert was a very wealthy man and had the financial means to purchase star players from cash-strapped Boston Red Sox owner, Harry Frazee. Ruppert's key acquisition was Babe Ruth. From 1921 until Ruppert's death in January 1939, the Yankees became the pre-eminent team in baseball. A family trust ran the team until it was sold to Dan Topping, Del Webb and Larry MacPhail in 1945. Two years later, MacPhail sold his interest to his partners, who owned the team until they sold it to CBS after the 1964 season.

Steinbrenner's accomplishments as Yankee owner totaled 11 pennants and seven championships (including 2009) and far exceeded those of his contemporaries. But under Ruppert (including the family trust), the Yankees won 14 American League pennants and 10 World Series. Topping and Webb, who relied on the expertise of general manager George Weiss for most of their tenure, boasted 15 pennants and 10 World Series in 20 years. The Boss certainly deserves credit for reviving the storied franchise, but it was Ruppert who made the deals that brought Babe Ruth to New York, which eventually caused Yankee Stadium to be built and launched the greatest dynasty in sports history.

Girardi Joins Selected Group

When Joe Girardi guided the Yankees to a World Series championship over the Phillies in 2009, he joined a select group of men who both played for and managed pennant-winning teams in the Bronx. Ralph Houk, a backup catcher in the 1940s and '50s, skippered the Yanks on three consecutive pennant winners from 1961 to 1963. Yogi Berra, a Yankee from 1947 to 1964, led the Yanks to a first-place finish as a player-manager in 1964. And Billy Martin, a second baseman in the 1950s, was at the helm when the Yanks captured two American League flags in 1976 and 1977. It's also worth noting that several former Yankee players who were pennant winners subsequently led other teams to a pennant.

And it's seldom mentioned, but Leo Durocher, who spent three seasons with the Yanks in the late 1920s, was a member of the 1928 championship team. As a manager, "Leo the Lip" led the Dodgers to the National League flag in 1941 and won two with the Giants (1951 and 1954), including their last championship in New York in 1954. Berra also managed the Mets to the National League pennant in 1973. Hank Bauer, who patrolled right field on nine pennant winners and seven championship teams with the Yanks from 1949 to 1958, was at the helm in Baltimore in 1966 as the Orioles swept the Dodgers, and Lou Piniella, an outfielder and designated hitter on four pennant winners and two championship teams from 1974 to 1981, guided the Cincinnati Reds to a win over Oakland in the 1990 Fall Classic.

Jeter a Stats Leader, and Legend

Not since Joe DiMaggio first stepped onto the field at Yankee Stadium in 1936 had the Yankees produced a homegrown player who performed at such a consistently high level for such a long time. Joltin' Joe's arrival in the Bronx coincided with the team's resurgence as a dominant power in Major League Baseball. They won six pennants and five World Series in DiMaggio's first seven years.

Similarly, when Derek Jeter joined the Yankees 60 years after DiMaggio's debut, there hadn't been a World Series played in the Bronx in 15 long years. It was the longest drought since before Babe Ruth arrived from Boston in the 1920s. The future Hall of Fame shortstop, who rooted for the Yankees as a kid growing up in Kalamazoo, Michigan, won over fans in his first full season. Jeter was a solid fielder and hit .314, winning the 1996 American League Rookie of the Year honors as New York won its first pennant since 1981 and first championship since 1978.

Jeter became a model of consistency as he hit .300 or better 12 times between 1996 and 2009, leading the Yankees to seven American League pennants and five World Series championships. As Ruth, Gehrig, DiMaggio and Mantle before him, Jeter became the face of the organization. He steadily climbed the team's all-time lists in several categories. His .312 lifetime average (as of August 2011) ranks fifth, behind Ruth (.342), Gehrig (.340), Earl Combs and DiMaggio (.325) and Bill Dickey (.313) for players with at least 5000 at-bats for the Yankees. And Jeter's seven seasons with 200 or more hits ranks second in Yankee history behind only Gehrig (eight seasons).

On August 16, 2009, Jeter hit a double against the Seattle Mariners for his 2675th hit and passed Hall of Famer Luis Aparicio for the most career hits for a shortstop in major league history. And he cemented his place in Yankees' lore three weeks later when he smashed career hit number 2722 to pass Gehrig as the storied franchise's all-time hits leader. And on July 9, 2011, he became the only Yankee to join the 3000-hit club. While the 37-year-old's best seasons are certainly behind him, Jeter will no doubt attain two more honors: enshrinement in the Hall of Fame in his first year of eligibility, and the last Yankee to ever wear a jersey with the number 2 on the back.

Chapter Two

Legends on Ice

The First Names on NHL Jerseys

When the National Hockey League (NHL) first decided to establish a franchise in the United States, they were taking a risk because most of the population had never seen a game of hockey. Canada, where the NHL was established, had invented the game, so it was the national pastime north of the border. In order to make the game easier for an American audience to understand and follow, the New York Americans were the first NHL team to put the players' last names on the backs of their jerseys during the 1925–26 season. It is a strange fact that the NHL did not make names on jerseys mandatory until 1978.

Buffalo Sabres

Malarchuk's Close Call

Hockey is a dangerous sport. Put 12, 200-pound men on razor-sharp blades and get them skating full bore on solid ice at incredible speeds, and someone is bound to get hurt. Over the years, players have had fractures of nearly every bone in their bodies, but rarely has a player been hurt by the most dangerous thing on the ice—the skate blades. The most famous incident involving a player being injured by another player's skate happened to Swedish-born Toronto Maple Leafs defenseman Börje Salming. During a game between the Maple Leafs and the Detroit Red Wings on November 26, 1986, Salming fell to the ice in front of his net and was accidentally cut by the blade of Red Wings forward Gerard Gallant. The injury required facial surgery and more that 200 stitches to close. Up to that point, the incident had been the most horrific skate injury in the history of hockey.

Then came a game between the Buffalo Sabres and St. Louis Blues on March 22, 1989, when Blues forward Steve Tuttle collided with a Sabres defenseman in front of the Buffalo net. Tuttle lost his balance, flipping his feet up off the ice. In a quick second, his blade sliced into Sabres goaltender Clint Malarchuk's neck, severing his jugular vein. Horrified fans looked on as Malarchuk grabbed his neck in a useless attempt to stop the blood from spilling all over the ice. In a matter of seconds, a large pool of blood had formed in front of Malarchuk, and had it not been for the quick thinking of Buffalo trainer Jim Pizzutelli, who applied pressure directly to the vein to slow the loss of blood, Malarchuk might have died right there on the ice. It took doctors 90 minutes and over 300 stitches to close the gash in his throat. Incredibly, Malarchuk returned a week later and for a game against the Quebec Nordiques.

But after the injury, Malarchuk was never the same. His performance declined, and he suffered from frequent nightmares because of the injury.

By a strange coincidence, another neck injury occurred in Buffalo when the Florida Panthers rolled into town to play the Sabres on February 10, 2008. Panthers forward Richard Zednik was cut in the neck by a teammate's skate, severing his external carotid artery. Zednik immediately skated over to the Florida bench, leaving a trail of blood on the ice. He was met by trainers and kept stable until he could be taken to a hospital. While not as serious as the Malarchuk incident, it was an eerie reminder of the dangers of the game.

Brother vs. Brother

In the history of the NHL, many brothers have played on the same team or against each other, but strangely, never before had there been a game where two brothers played against each other in goal. That is until March 20, 1971, when Dave Dryden of the Sabres was put in net against his younger brother Ken of the Montreal Canadiens. Both goaltenders had not been slated to play that night, but during the game, Canadiens goalie Rogie Vachon went down with an injury and was replaced by Ken Dryden. Immediately, Sabres head coach Punch Imlach pulled his goalie and put Dave in net. As the two brothers skated out onto the ice, the crowd cheered the historic event. "We were having a hamburger and kind of joked with each other, 'See you at center ice after we play tomorrow, ha ha,'" said Dave.

"It was really one of those unbelievable things. Our dad, who took the chance of driving to Montreal when it made no sense, was rewarded."

Ken ended up beating his brother in the game by a score of 5–2, but all of that didn't matter when the two met at center ice and shook hands. For the first time since they were kids playing street hockey, the Dryden brothers had played a game of hockey against each other. No other goaltending brothers have since equaled the achievement.

The French Connection

Gilbert Perreault, Rick Martin and René Robert were one of the most productive trios in the NHL during the mid-'70s. The "French Connection," as they became known, propelled the Buffalo Sabres into one of the top-tier teams in the league. Martin broke the 50-goal mark two years in a row, and both Perreault and Robert hit the 100-point mark over their careers.

The line was one of the major reasons why the Sabres finished the 1974–75 season at the top of the league in points and managed to beat the multi-talented Montreal Canadiens in the semi-finals to make their first trip to the Stanley Cup finals. Unfortunately, it was the defending Cup champion Philadelphia Flyers that came out on top, but the line of Perreault, Martin and Robert certainly didn't make the Flyers' job easy. Eventually, Robert was traded to the Colorado Rockies in 1979, and Martin suffered a career-ending knee injury in 1980.

Perreault, Buffalo's first-ever draft pick back in 1970, played all 17 of his seasons with the Sabres and was inducted into the Hockey Hall of Fame in 1990.

Sabres Miss the Cup by a Toe

For years, NHL players had been taking advantage of the lax attitude of referees toward goaltender interference, such as players crashing the net, sticking their behinds in goalies' faces and generally making it difficult for goaltenders to do their job. But by the late 1990s, goaltenders had had more than enough, and after much discussion with the NHL Players Association, the NHL board and the referees, it was decided that something had to be done. For the start of the 1998–99 season, the NHL added a new rule that stated:

> *Unless the puck is in the goal crease area, a player of the attacking side may not stand in the goal crease. If the puck should enter the net while such conditions prevail, the goal shall not be allowed. If an attacking player has physically interfered with the goalkeeper prior to or during the scoring of a goal…the goal will be disallowed and a penalty for goaltender interference will be assessed.*

To put it more simply, if a player's skate was in the blue-painted area and a goal was scored, it would be disallowed. That brief paragraph in the NHL rules set in motion a long and painful season of video-reviewed goals, angry coaches and frustrated players. The only players on the ice to benefit from this rule were the goalies, whose goals-against averages across the league fell the lowest they had been in years, with the top-four goalies in the league posting under 2.00 goals per game. Just two years earlier, not one goalie had even broken the 2.00 goals-against average.

Fans, owners and players all complained about the rule that slowed down the game with seemingly endless video reviews. It became something of a joke. If a player's foot was in the crease and wasn't even interfering with the goaltender, the goal was still disallowed. This strict adherence to the rules made players extra cautious around the nets, and as a consequence, fewer goals were scored. The league understood the complaints but decided to enforce the rule change through the playoffs to gage its full effect.

It all exploded in the league's face during the Stanley Cup finals when Buffalo played the Dallas Stars. Even with talented offensive players on both benches, the series was noted for its defensive play and for being a low-scoring affair. Therefore, every goal mattered even more. Buffalo had talented goaltender Dominik Hasek, but the Stars led the series after five games, three games to two. Game six was a must-win for Buffalo, a franchise that still has never won a Stanley Cup.

Once game six started, Dallas controlled the tempo, leading in puck possession and time spent in the opposition zone. But thanks to the goaltending of Hasek, regulation ended with the teams tied 2–2. Dallas pressed hard into the Sabres zone during the overtime period. The Stars piled several players in front of Hasek hoping to sneak a screened shot past him. When the shot from the point came in, Hasek still managed to get a piece of it, and the puck fell in the crease area. Stars forward Brett Hull swatted at the puck and managed to hit it into the back of the net.

The Stars piled off the bench and began celebrating their victory. The Sabres, however, had cause for complaint and immediately pleaded with referee Terry Gregson that Hull's skate was clearly in the crease at the time he put the puck into the net. However, Gregson made no effort to have the goal reviewed, and with that, the Sabres were robbed of their chance to win the Cup.

No one was more upset than Sabres head coach Lindy Ruff. "I wanted [NHL commissioner Gary] Bettman to answer the question why Hull's goal was not reviewed," said Ruff. "And really, he just turned his back on me like he knew this might be a tainted goal, and there was no answer for it."

The Sabres complaint was a valid one. During the regular season and playoffs, and right up until the moment that Hull swatted the puck into the net, that type of "goal" would have been disallowed. Adding insult to injury, just two days after the Stanley Cup final's controversial ending, NHL executives changed the crease violation rule. It was too little, too late for the Sabres, though, who have yet to return to the Stanley Cup finals.

Ruff Has the Right Stuff

Although the Sabres haven't won a Stanley Cup during the 14 years of coach Lindy Ruff's reign, Buffalo's ownership, the players and fans know they have a first-rate leader on the bench. The former defenseman spent his first 10 years in the NHL with Buffalo before he was traded to the New York Rangers near the end of the 1989 regular season. Ruff retired after two more campaigns in New York. He joined the Florida Panthers coaching staff in 1994 and left Miami when he returned to Western New York for the 1997–98 season as the head man in Buffalo. Ruff, who is the sixth former Sabres player to become head coach, led the team to their second Stanley Cup final in 1999.

Under Ruff, Buffalo has had 12 winning seasons in 13 years. He is the only coach in the history of the NHL's three New York teams to enjoy back-to-back, 50-win seasons (2005–06 and 2006–07). He is the winningest coach in franchise history, and his 526 victories with the Sabres are the most in NHL annals for a coach with the same team. Team management guaranteed that Ruff would improve those marks when they gave him a three-year contract extension in April 2011.

New York Islanders

Is There an Elephant in the Room?

Superstitions in the world of sports come in all forms. Some players eat the same meal before games; some put on equipment in a specific order;

some even abstain from amorous activities before games in the hope that it will provide them some sort of edge over the competition. As strange as some of these superstitions sound to those outside the sports world, even seasoned veterans were left shaking their heads when they heard of the 1975 New York Islanders' rather odd and smelly superstition.

In the opening round of the 1975 playoffs, the Islanders met their Patrick Division rivals the New York Rangers in a best-of-three series. It just so happened that Madison Square Garden, the Rangers home ice, was also hosting a circus on the off nights. It was the Islanders first trip to the playoffs since joining the league in 1972, and a friend of right-winger Billy Harris decided it would be a good idea to collect a heaping sample of elephant dung, seal it in a bag and give it to the team as a good-luck charm. Well, as luck would have it, the Islanders won the opening game 3–2. With elephant poo in hand, the Islanders went on to upset the Rangers and move onto a second-round series against the Pittsburgh Penguins.

The Penguins nearly put an end to the power of the good-luck feces by taking a 3–0 series lead. The only other team in the history of the NHL to come back from a 3–0 series deficit was the 1942 Toronto Maple Leafs against the Detroit Red Wings to win the Stanley Cup. With their lucky charm in hand, however, the Isles matched the Maple Leafs feat by winning the next four games straight.

The team, and the bag of poo, then traveled to Philadelphia to meet the defending champion Flyers in the semi-finals. Yet again, the Isles lost the first three games but then mounted an incredible comeback, winning the next three games to force a deciding game seven. Their luck, however, like the poop they carried around, had dried out. The Flyers won the final game 4–1 and went on to repeat as Stanley Cup champions. The bag of elephant poop was promptly tossed in the garbage, much to the relief of the less-superstitious players and anyone within the vicinity of the Islanders locker room.

"We had that Madison Square Garden aroma around us all the time from when we beat the Rangers," Islander defenseman Dave Lewis said. "And you thought playoff beards were weird?"

The Goaltender Scores!

Anyone who was a fan of the Islanders during their glory years in the early 1980s will tell you that one of the major reasons they were so successful was that they had goaltender Billy Smith, who was violently passionate about the game. A fierce competitor, Smith protected his net like it was his home. If any player dared get in his way, Smith was never afraid to let them know he was behind them with a quick stick chop to their legs. Most of the time, he performed his antics when the referee had turned away, but he was still caught often enough and earned himself a record number of penalty minutes for a goaltender. However, his tactics were effective.

"A goaltender has to protect his crease," Smith said. "If they're going to come that close, I have to use any means to get them out of there. If I have to use my stick, I'll use my stick."

Since joining the Islanders in 1972, Smith had been considered a good goaltender but not a great one. Then one incident occurred early in the 1979–80 season that made him believe that it was going to be a good year. Against the Colorado Rockies on November 28, 1979, the referee signaled a delayed penalty against the Islanders, and the Rockies pulled their goaltender for the extra attacker. Colorado pressed forward on the attack by shooting the puck deep into the Islanders zone, where the puck bounced off Smith's chest protector before quickly being picked up by Colorado's Rob Ramage. Under pressure from the Islanders defenders, Ramage made a quick blind pass back to the blue line in the hopes of hitting one of his teammates. Instead, no player was there to receive the pass, and the puck quickly shot down the ice directly toward the open Rockies net. Colorado players tried to stop the errant puck, but it slid right into their net. As the last of the Islanders to touch the puck, Billy Smith was credited with scoring the goal, making him the first goaltender in NHL history to "score" a goal.

From Olympic Gold to Stanley Cup

From the winter of 1980 through the spring of 1983, no player celebrated victory more than Ken Morrow of the New York Islanders. The defenseman from Flint, Michigan, was a member of the

U.S. Olympic hockey team that shocked the sporting world by upsetting the USSR team en route to winning a gold medal at the 1980 Winter Games in Lake Placid, New York. When the Olympics ended, many of the American players were eager to capitalize on their fame and signed with teams in the NHL. Morrow joined the New York Islanders, who had yet to win a Stanley Cup since they joined the NHL in 1970.

The 1980 Islanders that Morrow joined were still smarting from their premature elimination from the 1979 semi-finals at the hands of their Patrick Division rivals in Manhattan. Perhaps their new gold-medal-laden arrival was the good-luck charm the Isles needed. Morrow played in 18 regular-season games down the stretch, and the team streaked through the playoffs and won the first of four consecutive Stanley Cups when they beat Philadelphia in six games. Although Morrow never made the All-Star team during his 10 years in the league, all with the Islanders, he was a fan favorite and consistent contributor on one of the league's great dynasties.

New York Rangers

Boucher: Player, Coach, Gentleman

Hall of Fame centerman Frank Boucher was an original Ranger and one of the NHL's legendary players in its early years. Boucher, who was born in Ottawa, Ontario, in 1901, was just 5-foot-9 and 135 pounds. He was one of the great puck-handlers of his or any other era and an accurate passer; he led the league in assists three times. Boucher was part of the Blue Shirts' famous "Bread Line" along with the Cook brothers, Bill and Bun. With Boucher at center flanked by Bun on the left wing and Bill on the right, the trio led the Rangers to three Stanley Cup finals and the team's first two championships in 1928 and 1933.

Boucher was not only regarded as one of the league's best players, but he had also established a sterling reputation for his clean play on the ice. The center was awarded the Lady Byng Trophy seven times in eight seasons from 1928 to 1935. The trophy is named in honor of Marie Evelyn Moreton Byng, wife of Viscount Byng of Vimy, a Canadian World War I war hero who was the governor general of Canada from 1921 to 1926. Lady Byng, who was an avid hockey fan, donated the trophy in 1925 to the NHL player who was "adjudged to have exhibited the best type of sportsmanship and gentlemanly conduct combined with a high standard of playing ability." After Boucher had received the award the seventh and final time, Lady Byng also presented him with the original replica of the trophy and had a new one struck. No player has won the award more than Boucher. Legend Wayne Gretzky, who stands next on the list with five, won his final Lady Byng Trophy with the Rangers in 1999.

Boucher played 13 seasons and was later named Rangers coach. In his first season (1939–40), he guided the team to its third Stanley Cup championship. It would be their last until 1994. The Rangers were

77–47–20 in their first three seasons under Boucher, but a dismal 104–216–63 in his last eight. Hockey's first gentleman was inducted into the Hall of Fame in 1958 and died in Ottawa in 1977 at age 76.

Silver Fox to the Rescue

It played out like a scene in some Hollywood sports movie when New York Rangers head coach and manager Lester Patrick strapped on a pair of goalie pads and led his team to victory in a Stanley Cup finals playoff game and, at the same time, secured his place in the history of the game by providing one of hockey's most incredible stories.

It all happened during the 1928 Stanley Cup finals when Patrick's New York Rangers met the Montreal Maroons in game two of the best-of-five series. The regular Rangers netminder, Lorne Chabot, took a puck in the face early in the game (goalies weren't required to wear masks back then) and could not continue. The score at the time was 1–0 for the Rangers. In the old days of hockey, teams did not have backup goaltenders as they do today, forcing many goaltenders to play through all sorts of injuries, and if they could not continue, an emergency stand-in had to be found or else the team would have to forfeit the game.

Patrick knew that Ottawa Senators goaltender Alex Connell was in attendance watching the game and requested the permission of Maroons head coach Eddie Gerard to use the veteran goaltender in Chabot's place (because Connell played for another team, the Rangers had to get approval from the Maroons before they could enter him into the lineup). Naturally, the Maroons turned down that proposal, and Gerard suggested the Rangers try something else.

"Why not put Lester in the net if you need a goaltender that bad?" said Gerard.

Not willing to simply hand the victory over to the Maroons, Patrick responded, "I will, by God. I will!"

Disappearing into the Rangers dressing room, Patrick put on Chabot's equipment and skated out onto the ice to the disbelief of the crowd. Patrick had a long history of playing hockey prior to that game, but he had always played the forward position and had only tended the net during practices.

Despite his inexperience, Patrick performed remarkably well for a 44-year-old, silver-haired head coach. The Maroons tried all they could to put a puck past the "backup" goaltender, peppering shot after shot at the net, but Patrick held firm. In fact, he stopped all but one shot that beat him in the third period, forcing the game into overtime. Although a little tired, Patrick was up to the task and successfully defended his net until Rangers forward Frank Boucher scored the game winner. Although they had not yet won the Cup, the Rangers hoisted Patrick on their shoulders and paraded him around the arena like a conquering hero.

After the game, Patrick remarked on his performance, "I stopped only six or seven really hard shots.

My teammates saved the old man with their back checking." Luckily, the Rangers called up some help for the following game, and they went on to defeat the Maroons and win the franchise's first Stanley Cup.

The Cup Curse

When the New York Rangers first entered the NHL in 1926, they made it to the semi-finals of the playoffs only to be defeated by the Boston Bruins, but then won the Stanley Cup the following year. Another Stanley Cup followed in 1933, and when the Blue Shirts took home their third Cup in 1940, their fans had come to expect results from their team. Sure, they had their good and bad seasons, but up until 1940, they had produced solid results. Then the drought began, only to be broken 54 years later.

Some say the reason the Rangers spent all those years without a championship because of what happened on the night they won the 1940 Stanley Cup. Many devoted hockey fans, who can be quite superstitious, believe in the sanctity of the Stanley Cup, that a greater power oversees its well-being and that anything done to soil the Cup's purity will lead to supernatural repercussions—after all, the Cup is also known as "the Holy Grail" of hockey. The Rangers, caught up in celebration, forgot the Cup's sanctity for a moment and did something that placed a curse on the whole team.

In the locker room as players celebrated by taking turns drinking champagne from the bowl, Rangers president Colonel John Reed Kilpatrick decided it was the perfect time to commemorate the fully-paid mortgage on Madison Square Garden by setting fire to the deed in the bowl of Lord Stanley's Cup. In the eyes of the true believers of hockey's number-one symbol, the Rangers desecrated the trophy at that moment and cursed all the Rangers players and fans to a future without the Stanley Cup.

Over the next few decades, the Rangers only made it into the Stanley Cup finals twice and lost on both occasions. Despite having Hall of Fame players on their rosters through those years—players like Andy Bathgate, Chuck Rayner, Rob Gilbert, Gump Worsley, Ed Giacomin and Phil Esposito—they could never seem to find the right chemistry to take them to the championship.

Things were made worse for the Rangers faithful in the 1980s as they watched from the gutter of the NHL as their cross-town rivals, the New York Islanders, won four straight Stanley Cups. The Rangers had gone so long without a Cup that even the Islanders fans began to taunt them with chants of "1940" whenever they faced off against each other. Yet the Rangers fans held firm to their team through the bad years, and 54 years later, their patience finally paid off when "The Moose" came to town.

The Curse Is Over!

As the 1980s came to a close, the Rangers finally began to see some hope for the future. By 1990, the Rangers had established themselves as a top-tier team with two solid goaltenders in net (Mike Richter and John Vanbiesbrouck), the defensive talents of Brian Leetch, and most importantly, they had managed to sign four-time Stanley Cup–winner Mark Messier to the team.

By the end of the 1991–92 season, the new-look Rangers had vaulted to the top of the league, leading all teams for the first time since the 1941–42 season with a 50–25–5 record. But despite the strong finish that season, the curse once again reared its ugly head as the Rangers succumbed to the defending Stanley Cup champion Pittsburgh Penguins in the division finals in six games.

After posting the best record in the league that season, the Rangers finished in last place in their division and missed the playoffs the following year. Being a Rangers fan was becoming very difficult. Was it the curse coming back to haunt the Rangers after such a promising season? Were the Rangers ever going to win again? The players gave fans a reason to hope in the 1993–94 season when they came back with force once again, finishing the season with the best record in the league. But as any true Rangers fan knows, the curse has hung over their heads for 54 years and was not going to go away so easily. The first team to face the rejuvenated Rangers was their cross-town rivals, the New York Islanders.

Taunts of "1940" from the Islanders fans were quickly silenced as the Rangers cruised to an easy four-game sweep. The Rangers had an equally easy time with the Washington Capitals in the next round. The Capitals failed to mount any kind of offense in the series, unable to solve the Rangers defense and the stellar goaltending of Mike Richter, and were dispatched by the Blueshirts in five games. For the Conference finals against the New Jersey Devils, the Rangers were in tough, playing one of the strongest defensive teams in the league and facing one of the best young goaltenders in the game, Martin Brodeur.

Although the games were close, the Devils were able to take a 3–2 series lead and looked to finish off the Rangers on home ice in six games. New York newspaper headlines screamed that the curse had returned to yet again deny the Rangers of their best chance in decades to go all the way to the finals. "It wasn't like you could avoid it," said Rangers forward Nick Kypreos about the supposed lore of the curse. "It was everywhere—in the newspapers, on TV, from the fans."

But Rangers captain Mark Messier did not believe in curses and told his teammates in the dressing room before the start of game six that they would win the game and then win the series in seven. His words seemed rather hollow after the Devils staked out a quick 2–0 lead in the first period, but Rangers forward Alex Kovalev scored in the second to narrow the gap. Then it was Messier's turn to take control and prove that the curse could indeed be broken. Messier scored the tying goal, the game winner and, for the hat trick, an empty-net insurance goal to seal the victory. With the momentum on their side, the Rangers took game seven and moved into the Stanley Cup finals for only the third time since they last won the Cup. Their opponents were the Vancouver Canucks, who had made it to the finals for the first time.

While the Rangers had dominated the regular season atop the league, the Canucks had spent the entire season on the edge of missing out on the playoffs and just managed to sneak in at the last moment. Vancouver surprised the Rangers with a series-opening victory, but the Canucks then lost the next three straight games, placing them one game away from losing out on the Cup. All of New York was abuzz at the possibility that the Rangers would finally bring the Stanley Cup back to the city after a 54-year absence. With a 3–1 series lead, the curse was the farthest thing from fans' minds. But when the Rangers lost the next two games, forcing the series into a deciding game seven, the curse had magically resurfaced.

Game Seven and the Cup

Back in Madison Square Garden for game seven, the Rangers could not shake the feeling that the curse was about to once again ruin their chance at Stanley Cup glory. Despite the distinct possibility of watching their team lose the Stanley Cup, fans packed the seats, holding onto a faint hope that their team could pull off a miracle. The teams traded a couple of goals, but it was the Rangers who went late into the third period with a 3–2 lead. As the minutes and seconds on the clock ticked off and the Stanley Cup waited in the wings, no one in the building dared to celebrate until the final buzzer had sounded. An odd hush fell over the Garden as the Canucks pressed into the Rangers zone late in the period and rang a puck off the post behind goaltender Mike Richter, but that was as close as the Canucks would come. The final buzzer sounded, ending the 54-year curse and sending the crowd into a frenzy of pent-up excitement. The Rangers jumped off the bench and onto the ice for a long-overdue celebration.

"For guys like Mike Richter, Brian Leetch and Messier, who truly carried the Cup burden, winning as unbelievable, like a 5000-pound weight being lifted," said right-winger Nick Kypreos. For the fans of the Rangers who had stuck by them through all the bad years, it was truly a moment worth waiting for—but just don't ask them to do it again.

Number 99 Has Left the Building

We all knew that the day would eventually come when Wayne Gretzky would hang up his skates, but it hardly seemed real since, in his 20 years as an NHL player, he seemed immortal. Looking back at his career that passed through Edmonton, Los Angeles and St. Louis before finally ending up in New York with the Rangers, Gretzky had put together one of the most incredible individual chapters in the history of the game. But letting go of that incredible legacy was not going to be easy for his fans or for the "Great One" either.

By the late 1990s, Gretzky had become much less effective offensively than he once was as a young point-scoring machine with the Edmonton Oilers, but he still managed to place in the top-five scorers in the league most seasons. Many people felt the Great One still had a few good seasons left in his skates, but the hockey world could sense that Gretzky was getting very close to calling it quits.

Although he had yet to announce his retirement, fans across the league paid tribute to the Great One like he was on his farewell tour. In arenas across the league near the end of the 1998–99 season, fans rose from their seats at the end of the games and applauded Gretzky for all that he had done for the game and for all his accomplishment. In places like Philadelphia, Montreal, Pittsburgh, Edmonton and St. Louis, whenever the Rangers rolled into town, hockey fans clamored to get one last glimpse of the Great One. Even with all the rumors swirling about and the end of the season fast approaching, Gretzky still had yet to formerly announce his plans. However, with one game left in the season, Gretzky finally spoke to the press and told the hockey world the news that it never wanted to hear.

His last game was to be played in Madison Square Garden on Sunday, April 18, 1999, against the Pittsburgh Penguins, the final game of the season given that the Rangers had failed to make the playoffs.

Despite pleas from his family and friends not to leave the game, the 38-year-old Gretzky said he had a feeling that it was time to call it quits. "The last couple of weeks, a lot of people have been asking me why this is the time," said a composed Gretzky during a press conference the day before his final game. "It's a gut feeling, something I believe is right. I started to feel fatigue—mentally and physically—that I never felt before."

Even knowing that it was time did not make the decision any easier for the Great One. "I hate the fact I have to retire," he said. "I have played for 35 years, since I was three. Now I'm handing in my skates—I'm done."

During that final game at Madison Square Garden, the entire hockey world watched for the last time as number 99 jumped over the boards, handled the puck and took a slap-shot on net in that oh-so-Gretzky manner. For good measure, the Great One even got an assist on a Brian Leetch goal, but as the clock ticked down, Gretzky finally began to realize the enormity of the moment. "[During a final Rangers timeout], I looked up and said, 'My goodness, I've got 30 seconds to go.' That's when it hit me," he said.

When the buzzer finally did go off, it put an end to a career that had spanned 1487 games through 20 seasons. Gretzky's career totals of 894 goals and 1963 assists for 2857 points are not only tops in all three categories, but the second-ranked players in each statistic are far behind. Added to that are 382 playoff points scored in pursuit of four Stanley Cups and an incredible 60 scoring records.

Four times, Gretzky came out of the dressing room to salute the crowd, while he collected the dozens of flowers and gifts that rained down onto the ice in tribute. When he finally mustered the will to pull himself off the ice for the last time, he could not bring himself to remove his jersey. "It's hard. I'll be honest. I don't want to take it off," he told the crowd of reporters who surrounded him in the locker room. But when he finally pulled it off, the jersey was quickly packed off to the Hockey Hall of Fame and the Great One said goodbye to hockey for good. In 1999, we said goodbye to 99.

Chapter Three

College All-Stars

The Heisman

Anyone who knows anything about football knows that the Heisman Trophy is given out annually to the season's most outstanding college football player. However, few people know anything about the man who gave his name to the trophy, John William Heisman.

Born in Cleveland, Ohio, in 1869, John Heisman played football through his high school and university days at Brown and the University of Pennsylvania, but it was as a coach where he would leave his mark, lending his expertise to a generation of athletes and helping establish a sporting tradition among American colleges. From 1892 to 1927, John Heisman coached baseball and basketball but was most widely known as a football coach. In his football career as a coach, he was the brain behind seven university teams holding an incredible 186 wins, 70 losses and 18 ties.

After retiring from his coaching career in 1927, he moved to New York City, where he became the athletic director of the Downtown Athletic Club. In 1935, the organization issued a trophy to be awarded to the best college football player. However, when Heisman died on October 3, 1936, the Downtown Athletic Club renamed the trophy the Heisman Memorial Trophy in his honor. Up until 2002, the Downtown Athletic Club handed out the trophy, but after its bankruptcy, the Yale Club in New York City took over awarding the trophy.

Sowing the Seeds of Victory

The afternoon of May 18, 1901, was a memorable one for a former baseball player. As he would recall a half-century later, his school was tied with their traditional rivals 3–3 in the ninth inning:

> *I worked the pitcher for a base on balls. I was no Ty Cobb, but in those days I could run. So I was off on the first pitch. Sure enough, the catcher threw wild and I kept going. The ball was heaved over the third baseman's head and I trotted home with what proved to be the winning run.*

The batter in question never played pro ball, but his derring-do on the base paths still meant so much to him years later because it was the first baseball game ever played between West Point and Annapolis. The young cadet who scored the winning run that day returned to West Point 20 years later as the commandant of the academy. His love of athletics and the character he believed that was developed in competition inspired him to compose the following adage: "Upon the fields of friendly strife are sown the seeds that upon other fields, on other days, will bear the fruits of victory." That phrase is inscribed on the walls of the gymnasium to this day. The author's name is Douglas MacArthur.

World War II Heroes

Several West Point cadets distinguished themselves on the athletic fields years before they became household names during World War II. Class of 1909 graduate George Patton competed in the modern pentathlon at the 1912 Olympics. The man, who later led the American Seventh Army to victory in Sicily and drove the U.S. Third Army to even greater heights as the Allies vanquished the Germans in France and Germany, finished fifth overall as he competed in 300-meter freestyle swimming, fencing, horse riding, pistol shooting and the four-kilometer run. Patton qualified for the pentathlon again for the 1916 Olympics scheduled for Berlin, but the Games were canceled because of World War I.

The Class the Stars Fell On

The West Point class of 1915 saw 59 of its graduates attain the rank of general, and several of the cadets were exceptional athletes. James Van Fleet starred on Army's undefeated football team. After serving in World War I, Van Fleet ran the Reserve Officers' Training Corps program at the University of Florida and also served as the school's football coach in 1923–24, leading the Gators to a 12–3–4 record. Van Fleet was eventually promoted to general during World War II and served under George Patton in the Third Army.

Omar Bradley was an excellent baseball player for the Black Knights of the Hudson and sometimes played semi-pro ball. He was acknowledged as one of the best players in the nation during his junior and senior seasons, excelling as both a hitter and out-fielder. Bradley served in both World Wars and became one of only five men during World War II to attain the rank of General of the Army. After the war, he was selected by President Truman to be the first Chairman of the Joint Chiefs of Staff.

Another class of '15 standout helped popularize the game of golf. He even had a putting green built outside the home office that he worked out of at 1600 Pennsylvania Avenue in Washington, DC. As much as he loved golfing, Dwight Eisenhower said one of his greatest athletic achievements occurred as a member of Army's football team, when he laid an open-field tackle on legendary Jim Thorpe in a game against Carlisle.

Heisman's on the Hudson

In the 85 years that the Downtown Athletic Club awarded the Heisman Trophy to the top college foot-ball player in the county, only four have been won by players from New York schools. Syracuse standout Ernie Davis won the Heisman in 1961. The other three recipients played at the U.S. Military Academy.

In 1945, Felix Anthony "Doc" Blanchard became the first of West Point's three Heisman winners. As a junior, he was the first-ever underclassman to win the award. A year later, Blanchard's backfield mate Glenn Davis also won the award. Blanchard was known as "Mr. Inside" while Davis was called "Mr. Outside," and together the pair became one of the most lethal tandems in college football history. During their three years starring for the Black Knights, the team went 27–0–1, with their lone blemish a 0–0 tie in 1946 against Notre Dame at Yankee Stadium.

Army's third and final Heisman winner was Pete Dawkins in 1958. Dawkins, who also starred on the academy's hockey team, was one of the top cadets in his class and, upon graduation, was awarded a prestigious Rhodes scholarship to Oxford University in England. The career soldier rose to the rank of general before retiring from the army in 1983.

Short Man Plays Tall

Calvin Murphy of Norwalk, Connecticut, was a highly recruited basketball player during his senior season of high school basketball in 1966. The 5-foot-9 world-class ball handler and scoring machine was visited by representatives from most major programs, including UCLA, which at the time was becoming the premier Division I school under coach John Wooden. But all the big schools were so deep in talent that Murphy was told he'd receive limited playing time until his junior or senior season. It was on a recruiting trip to Niagara University where he witnessed the intensity of the Purple Eagles rivalry with nearby St. Bonaventure that Murphy decided that sitting on the bench wasn't for him.

At Niagara, a small Catholic school that overlooks the Niagara River gorge just five miles past the famed Falls, Murphy was a three-time All-American as he averaged 33 points per game and set nearly every school scoring record by the time he graduated in 1970. During his senior season, he led Niagara to the NCAA tournament, then just 32 teams, where it advanced to the second round before losing to Villanova.

He was a second-round pick of the then–San Diego Rockets, who eventually moved to Houston. He made the NBA All-Rookie Team and became an All-Star in the 1979 season and set many team records during a 14-year career all spent with the Rockets franchise. He is regarded as one of the greatest free-throw shooters in league history. During the 1980–81 campaign, he set a then-record of hitting 78 consecutive shots from the line. When Murphy retired following the 1983 season, his career .892 free-throw percentage, which currently ranks seventh all time, was second only to teammate Rick Barry's .900. Murphy, who was also a national baton-twirling champion, was elected into the Basketball Hall of Fame in 1993. He is the shortest player in the Hall of Fame of a sport dominated by tall men.

Big Feet Accomplished Great Feats

In 1964, Bob Lanier tried out for the basketball team at Bennett High School in Buffalo because some of his friends did. Although some of them made the final cut, the very tall, gawky high school sophomore was unceremoniously cut—the coach told him he was too clumsy and would never become a basketball player. While his buddies played for Bennett, a determined Lanier improved his athletic skills and began learning the finer points of the game at a local Boys and Girls Club. The kid, whose feet would grow to size 22—yes, 22—eventually became the city champion in table tennis. Luckily for Lanier, and to the dismay of his future college and NBA opponents, Bennett hired a new hoops coach for Lanier's junior season and he made the team, quickly becoming one of the top players in Western New York.

He was heavily recruited by major college programs but wanted to stay near home. It was Lanier's father who made the final decision for Bob to accept a scholarship to St. Bonaventure, a small Catholic school about an hour's drive south of Buffalo. In his sophomore year, the three-time All-American led the Bonnies to the 1968 NCAA tournament. After a one-year ban from the tournament as the result of a recruiting violation, St. Bonaventure advanced to the Final Four before losing to eventual runner-up Jacksonville State (Florida), which was powered by Artis Gilmore. Lanier suffered a leg injury in a regional game, preventing him from his showdown with Gilmore.

Lanier, at 6-foot-11, was the number-one overall pick in the 1970 NBA draft. He spent 10 years with the Detroit Pistons before being traded to the Milwaukee Bucks. The eight-time NBA All-Star, whose number 16 was retired by both teams, averaged 20 points over his 14-year career and has been honored on several occasions by the NBA and civic associations for his charitable work. In 1992, he was elected into the Basketball Hall of Fame, and the basketball court at St. Bonaventure bears the name of the school's greatest player.

Syracuse's Royal Succession at Running Back

Perhaps no college in NCAA Division I history produced four great running backs in such a short span as Syracuse did from 1954 to 1968. Under head coach Ben Schwartzwalder, the program rose to national prominence thanks to the running of Jim Brown, Ernie Davis, Floyd Little and Larry Csonka. The Orangemen went 98–38–2 and finished in the post-season top-20 poll 10 times, including their national championship team of 1959 that capped an 11–0 season with a 23–14 win over Texas in the Cotton Bowl. All four are in the College Football Hall of Fame, and Brown, Little and Csonka are also in the Pro Football Hall of Fame. Davis, who died before he suited up in the pros, won the Heisman Trophy in 1961.

Brown Sets a High Standard

Jim Brown, considered one of the greatest all-around athletes in American history, was a four-sport star at Manhasset High School on Long Island in the early 1950s. He earned 13 varsity letters in football, basketball, baseball and lacrosse. His two no-hitters as a pitcher caught the attention of the Yankees, who offered the teen sensation a $150,000 signing bonus. He was heavily recruited by many major

Division I programs but chose Syracuse because one of his mentors, Kenneth Molloy, had played lacrosse at the school.

Brown, like Davis, Little and Csonka who followed him, only played three seasons on the varsity team, because at the time, freshmen were ineligible to play. Once he was able to suit up, he became a star in football, basketball, lacrosse and track. Wearing number 44, Brown was the third leading rusher in the nation his senior season. His most memorable performance came against Colgate, when he ran for 196 yards and scored six touchdowns, one two-point conversion and booted five extra points. He was a unanimous All-America selection in 1956 and finished fifth in the Heisman Trophy voting.

In lacrosse, Brown scored 30 goals his junior season in 1956 and added 43 goals and 21 assists his senior year, earning first-team All-America honors as a midfielder as the Orangemen went 10–0. His final game was particularly noteworthy as Syracuse hosted powerhouse Army, who they had not beaten in 18 years, with the national championship at stake. Brown scored one goal and added three assists as Syracuse beat Army 8–6 for the championship and completed its first undefeated season since 1922. What made Brown's performance exceptional is that the game was played on the same field immediately following Syracuse's victory over Colgate in a dual track meet. Against Colgate that day, Brown won the high jump and javelin and placed second in the discus. In Brown's final lacrosse game, he scored five goals, all in the first half, of the 1957 North–South Collegiate All-Star game.

Brown was a first-round pick of the Cleveland Browns in 1957. He led the NFL in rushing in eight of his nine seasons, including the team's championship season of 1964. He set many single-game, single-season and career rushing records and retired as the league's all-time leading rusher (12,365 yards) following the 1965 season at age 29. Brown is a member of the Pro Football Hall of Fame, the College Football Hall of Fame and the Lacrosse Hall of Fame. He is still regarded by those who saw him play as the greatest football and lacrosse player ever.

All-American, All-Around Great Guy

Ernie Davis' athletic career is full of triumphs but ended in tragedy. Davis was a great all-around athlete who grew up in Elmira, New York, less than a two-hour drive south of Syracuse. He starred in football and basketball at Elmira Free Academy, where Orangemen football coach Ben Schwartzwalder made many recruiting trips in that autumn of 1957. The 6-foot-2, 210-pound Davis broke into the starting backfield in 1959 and led the team in rushing with 686 yards and 10 touchdowns. Syracuse finished the regular season 10–0 and went to the Cotton Bowl, where Davis scored two touchdowns in a 23–14 win over Texas to give the school its only national championship.

The "Elmira Express" was the team's offensive threat in 1960 and 1961, winning All-America honors both years. In 1960, he rushed for 877 yards, averaging 7.8 yards per carry. He closed out his career a year later, gaining 823 yards on the ground (5.5 per carry) and scoring 15 touchdowns, including one on an interception return. In his final college football game, Davis gained 140 yards on 30 carries in a 15–14 win over Miami in the Liberty Bowl. Nobody was surprised when Davis was awarded the Heisman Trophy. He was the first African American to win the award, given annually to the nation's top college football player.

Athletic success brought fame, but one thing Ernie Davis didn't need was more friends. He was one of the nicest people and most admired students at the university. People back home in Elmira felt the same way. He wasn't just a gentleman, but a gentle man. Davis was selected by the Washington Redskins in the first round of the 1962 draft, but Cleveland owner Art Model dreamed of teaming Davis with Syracuse alumnus Jim Brown to form a "Dream Backfield." So Cleveland dealt future Hall of Famer Bobby Mitchell and a number-one pick for Davis, and Model signed his new jewel to a multi-year contract by Christmas.

But in training camp that summer, Davis became ill and was diagnosed with leukemia. He started treatments immediately but died on May 18, 1963, at age 23. Davis made such a positive impression on Model that the Cleveland owner retired Davis' number 45 jersey even though he never played a single down for the Browns. Elmira honored its hometown hero by renaming the high school after him. At Syracuse, the university named a dormitory for Davis and erected a statue of his likeness; the football team now plays its home games at Ernie Davis Legends Field.

Little Raises the Bar

Like Jim Brown and Ernie Davis before him, Floyd Little wore number 44 at Syracuse. And as high as Brown and Davis set the bar, the New Haven, Connecticut, native raised it even higher when he became the school's first, and still only, three-time All-American from 1964 to 1966. The 5-foot-11, 195-pound Little placed fifth in the Heisman Trophy voting his junior and senior seasons. In 1965, he became the first Syracuse running back to rush for more than 1000 yards (1065), and he holds the school record for career touchdowns (46) and punt returns for touchdowns (5). In his final game as an Orangeman, Little rushed for a school-record 216 yards against Tennessee in the Gator Bowl and graduated as the Orangemen's all-time leading rusher (2704).

Little was the Denver Broncos first-round pick and enjoyed five Pro Bowl seasons on mostly losing teams in the Mile High City. His 5566 yards gained on the ground was the most in the NFL from 1968 to 1973. Little, who earned a law degree from the University of Denver, retired after the 1975 season as the NFL's seventh-ranked ground gainer in history with 6323 yards. He was elected into the College Football Hall of Fame in 1983 and Pro Football Hall of Fame in 2010.

Csonka Rambled, Defenders Rolled

Outside of his exceptional ability to move the pile forward, nobody would compare Larry Csonka to his three All-American predecessors. What "The Zonk" lacked in speed and moves, he more than made up for with straight-ahead power. At 6-foot-3, 240 pounds, he starred in the backfield for two seasons with Floyd Little before winning All-America honors himself in 1967.

He was a first-round pick of Miami in 1968 and became the featured running back in Don Shula's offense that powered the Dolphins to three consecutive Super Bowls and two championships. He was an All-Pro five times and set a then–Super Bowl, single-game rushing record when he ran for 145 yards against the Vikings in Super Bowl VIII. His MVP performance against the Vikings makes him the only former Syracuse player to win that award.

He spent nine of his eleven years in Miami; there were also two dismal seasons with the Giants before he retired as the NFL's fifth-ranked all-time rusher with 8081 yards. Csonka, who enjoyed three seasons with 1000-plus yards rushing, was elected into the Pro Football Hall of Fame in 1986. He was the first Orangeman to gain more than 1000 yards in two seasons, rushing for 1012 and 1127 yards in 1966 and 1967, respectively. He finished with 14 100-yard rushing performances and ended his collegiate career as the school's top ground gainer (2934). More than four decades since Csonka left Syracuse, he still ranks third on the career rushing list behind Joe Morris (4299), who went on to star with the Giants in the 1980s, and Walter Reyes (3424), who played from 2001 to 2004. Floyd Little is ranked fifth and Ernie Davis is 10th.

Nance a Two-sport Star

Although Jim Nance didn't win a Heisman Trophy or get enshrined in the Pro Football Hall of Fame, he did leave a great legacy at Syracuse as well as in pro football. Following the departure of Davis, Nance became the featured back in Syracuse's running attack as a sophomore in 1962. He was a three-year starter, and in his senior year, he tied Jim Brown's school mark of 13 touchdowns in a season. Nance wasn't an All-American on the gridiron, but he did earn that distinction by winning the NCAA wrestling championship in the heavyweight division in 1963 and 1965. He was the first African American grappler to win the heavyweight crown.

Nance played for the Boston Patriots of the AFL in 1966, where he set a single-season rushing mark of 1458 yards. He also led the league in touchdowns (11) and was voted the league's Most Valuable Player. A year later, the 6-foot-1, 240-pound full back gained a league-leading 1216 yards and became the first AFL runner to break the 1000-yard mark twice. Unfortunately, injuries hampered the rest of his career. After seven seasons with the Patriots and one with the Jets, he retired after the 1973 season. Nance, who died in 1992 at age 49, was elected into the Patriots Hall of Fame in 2009.

Chapter Four

The Ponies, the Links and the Net

Horseracing

Chenery's Two-year-old Shows Promise

Secretariat's debut as a two-year-old horse came on July 4, 1972, at Aqueduct Racetrack in Queens. Owner Penny Chenery's chestnut colt was favored to win but finished a disappointing fourth in the 5½-furlong race. Eleven days later, he broke his maiden in a 6-furlong race at Aqueduct. His only other defeat that season came via disqualification, in which he was placed second for bumping in the Champagne Stakes at Belmont. Nevertheless, trainer Lucien Laurin and jockey Ron Turcotte guided the horse Chenery had nicknamed "Big Red" to seven total victories in nine races that summer and captured the Horse of the Year Award, the first two-year-old to earn that honor.

Secretariat's Spectacular

There's only three weeks between the second and third leg of Thoroughbred Horse Racing's Triple Crown races, the Preakness and Belmont Stakes.

Secretariat won the Kentucky Derby in record time then took the Preakness by 2½ lengths. Only chronic doomsayers were expecting a contest at Belmont Park when owner Penny Chenery's prize chestnut colt attempted to become the first horse in 25 years to win all three Triple Crown races.

Jockey Ron Turcotte had to deal with "Secretariat Mania" that was sweeping the nation. Big Red was featured on the covers of *Time*, *Newsweek* and *Sports Illustrated* the week of the June 9th race. The 1973 Belmont Stakes was the most watched horseracing event in history. It wasn't a question whether Secretariat would win, but by how much. When Turcotte guided the horse into the gate, gamblers had established him an unheard of 1-to-10 betting favorite against a field of only four competitors.

Secretariat broke from the gate and set a fast pace. Sham, which had placed second in the Kentucky Derby and the Preakness, hung with the betting favorite as the pair pulled away from the field. But as Secretariat picked up the pace, Sham faded and eventually finished last. Meanwhile, Turcotte was atop a horse that was pulling away from the field as the crowd of nearly 70,000 was on its feet cheering. As horse and jockey came down the stretch, it was clear the sporting world was viewing an epic performance. Secretariat, as one observer noted, was no longer racing other horses, he was racing against himself and history. He crossed the wire at 2:24, not only a record for the Belmont but also the fastest 1½ miles on dirt in history. And the 31-length margin of victory

(248 feet) was also a record, beating the mark of 25 lengths set by Triple Crown–winner Count Fleet in 1943. Four decades later, Big Red's record for time and margin of victory in the Belmont still stands. The horse, and that day, won't soon be forgotten.

Woody's Hot Streak

Legendary trainer Woody Stephens' horses won a record five consecutive Belmont Stakes winners from 1982 to 1986. The winners were, in order: Conquistador Cielo, Caveat, Swale, Creme Fraiche and Danzig Connection. Stephens also trained two Kentucky Derby winners, Cannonade (1974) and Swale (1984). His lone Preakness winner was Blue Man in 1952. In a career that spanned seven decades, Stephens won more than 100 Grade 1 Stakes races. In 1983, Stephens finally received acknowledgment for his outstanding achievements when he won the Eclipse Award for Outstanding Trainer. Eclipse awards are given annually in 20 thoroughbred horseracing categories and are sponsored by the National Thoroughbred Racing Association (NTRA), Daily Racing Form and the National Turf Writers Association. The Stanton, Kentucky, native was elected into the National Museum of Racing and Hall of Fame in Saratoga Springs in 1976 and died in 1996 at age 84.

Golf

The Master of Flash and Substance, Too

During the "Golden Age of Sports" in the 1920s, Walter Hagen was to golf what Babe Ruth was to baseball. Before the Rochester native arrived on the scene, golf was a sport played mostly by rich people at country clubs. Hagen, who was born in 1892 to immigrant parents—his father was German and his mother Irish—helped raised the status of early golf pros from country club instructors to the megastars they are today.

It was at Rochester's country clubs that he learned how to play golf—but as a caddy and not a club member. Like his friend Ruth, Sir Walter was flashy—he often arrived at tournaments in a limo wearing a tuxedo—boisterous, quotable and very, very good at his chosen sport. He won the U.S. Open twice, the British Open four times (he was the first American to win that tournament) and the PGA five times, including four consecutive wins from 1924 to 1927. Throughout his career, "The Haig" was known for outdueling the other big names in the sport such as Ben Hogan, Byron Nelson and Sam Snead. But when he wasn't competing against the world's top golfers, Hagen was often on the road living the high life as a touring professional, giving public exhibitions as well as private lessons. He was the first high-profile golfer to make a substantial living as a professional golfer. His success may not have made him a millionaire, he said, but it allowed him to "live like one."

In 1926, Hagen challenged top amateur Bobby Jones to a pair of 36-hole matches under "match-play" rules. Hagen's game was the perfect description of the kind of golfer who could give the reserved Jones fits. Hagen loved to talk to his opponents and joke with the crowd, while the man who would one day conceive the Masters Tournament was quiet, businesslike and could become frustrated quickly. The best professional and top amateur squared off in what was considered at the time to be the "Match of the Century," in Sarasota and St. Petersburg, Florida. Hagen beat Jones 12-and-11 (12 holes up with 11 to play), a very large margin of victory, and considered it his career highlight.

The success of the blue-collar kid from western New York helped popularize golf with the masses. Slowly but steadily, the stuffy world of competitive golf gave way to the big-time professional tour that it is today. Hagen's style and dash won over the media, his personality won over fans and his greatness on the golf course, along with his vision, changed the sport of golf forever.

A Little Man with a Big Swing

Sixteen years before Bobby Thomson's pennant-winning home run at the Polo Grounds sent the New York Giants to the World Series, golfer Gene Sarazen hit a shot on the 15th hole of the final round of the 1935 Masters tournament that legendary sportswriter Grantland Rice dubbed, "The Shot Heard Round the World." Actually, Rice should have called it, "The Shot 'Heard About' Round the World." It occurred in the pre-televison era and only eight people witnessed it since Sarazen was trailing leader Craig Wood, who had already finished his final round, by three strokes. Sarazen was proud that two of the witnesses were Glen Hagen and Bobby Jones. The 5-foot-6 Sarazen's four-wood "double-eagle" on the 485-yard, par-five hole went in from 235 yards to tie him with Wood. He parred his last three holes then beat Wood by five strokes in a 36-hole playoff the next day.

In winning the 1935 Masters, Sarazen—who was born Gene Saracini but changed his name because he didn't like the way it looked in the newspaper—became the first golfer to win all four Grand Slam tournaments of the modern era. Born to Italian immigrant parents in Harrison, about 30 miles north of New York City, Sarazen's introduction to golf came as a caddy. Known as "The Squire," Sarazen won a total of seven Grand Slam events throughout his career and enjoyed rivalries with Hagen and Jones. He turned pro at age 19 and won the first of his two U.S. Open and PGA championships in 1922 when he was 20. Along with his lone Masters victory, The Squire finished with two U.S. Open wins, three PGAs and one British Open (1932).

Parting Shot, Heard Round the World

One of professional golf's best qualities is the reverence it shows to past champions. They're often allowed to participate in the qualifying rounds of tournaments when their competitive days are way behind them. In 1973, Sarazen played in the British Open on the 50th anniversary of his first appearance. It's a shame that the legendary sportswriter Grantland Rice wasn't alive and covering the Open that year. One wonders what the famed wordsmith would have written when the 71-year-old Sarazen, swinging five-iron, made a hole-in-one on the par-three, eighth hole at the Royal Troon Golf Course in Scotland.

Tennis

Mac and Mary

Although John McEnroe earned his place in the Hall of Fame as a dominating singles player, he entered the tennis world's upper echelon first as part of a mixed doubles team. As an 18-year-old amateur still in high school, McEnroe teamed with fellow New Yorker Mary Carillo to win the mixed doubles title at the 1977 French Open. It would be the only title he ever won at Roland Garros. Two months later, "Johnny Mac" advanced to the semifinals of the men's singles at Wimbledon, where he lost to Jimmy Connors in four sets. It was the best performance by an amateur at a Grand Slam tournament in the open era. The kid from Douglaston, Queens, had arrived.

In 1979, he won three Grand Slam titles, including the U.S. Open men's singles title, and he spent the next five years making the lives of opponents—and tennis officials—pure hell. From 1979 to 1984, he won four U.S. Open singles titles and three men's singles titles at Wimbledon. He also won four of his five Wimbledon doubles titles and four U.S. Open doubles titles during that span. Johnny Mac's excellence on the court was somewhat diminished by his boorish behavior during tournaments. The targets of his temper tantrums were not opposing players, but the line and chair umpires.

Besides interrupting play, McEnroe's infamous out-bursts often resulted in his being penalized and fined.

The 1977 French Open pairing was the high-water career mark for Mary Carillo, who was part of the women's tour from 1977 to 1980. Shortly after retiring, the Queens native became a television analyst and today is generally regarded as one of the best and most authoritative media personalities covering tennis.

Graf Wins First Open and Completes Grand Slam

Steffi Graf was having a banner year even before she beat Gabriela Sabatini (6–3, 3–6, 6–1) in the women's final of the 1988 U.S. Open to become just the third woman in the Open era to win the Grand Slam. Like professional golf, tennis has four major tournaments that are considered Grand Slam events: the Australian Open, the French Open, Wimbledon and the U.S. Open. Several men and women have won all of the Grand Slam tournaments over their careers, but only a few have won them all in one season. Graf beat Chris Evert in straight sets at the Australian Open (6–1, 7–6), then she topped Natasha Zvereva (6–0, 6–0) at the French Open, before battling past Martina Navratilova (5–7, 6–2, 6–1) at Wimbledon. The German sensation, who was just 19 when she defeated Sabatini at Flushing Meadows for the first of her eventual five Open singles titles, joined Maureen Connolly (1952) and Margret Smith-Court (1970) as the only women to win all four tournaments in one season.

Austin's a "Sweet 16" Sensation

Chris Evert advanced to the finals of the 1979 U.S. Open expecting to win her fifth consecutive women's singles crown at Flushing Meadows. Her opponent that day was Tracy Austin, who was making her first appearance in a Grand Slam final. Austin upset the 24-year-old Evert (6–4, 6–3) and, in doing so at age 16 years and 9 months, became the youngest player, male or female, to win the event. Austin's second singles championship was a grueling affair in which she defeated Martina Navratilova (1–6, 7–6(4), 7–6) in 1981.

Austin, who is the sister-in-law of fitness guru Denise Austin, won a third Grand Slam event in 1980 when she teamed with her brother, John, to win the mixed doubles final at Wimbledon. Unfortunately, chronic back problems cut her career short and she never won another Grand Slam event.

Chapter Five

Knicks and Nets

New York Knicks

Oh, Captain, My Captain!

Long Island poet Walt Whitman opened his famous poem about the death of Abraham Lincoln with "Oh Captain, My Captain!" The fans of the New York Knicks who followed the team during its first championship season in 1969–70 felt the same way toward the on-the-court leader of the NBA's Eastern Division champions, Willis Reed. The starting lineup that coach Red Holzman sent out each game featured guards Walt Frazier and Dick Barnett and forwards Dave DeBusschere and Bill Bradley, all of whom were good offensive shooters who could step in and fill the void if someone was having a poor night. But it was the man in the middle who held it all together. Standing just under 6-foot-10, the 245-pound Reed was a threat both at scoring and crashing the boards. He had a good jumper and relished battling the likes of Wilt Chamberlain, Wes Unseld, Bill Russell and Nate Thurmond for rebounds.

The team's captain led the unit in both categories that season, but Frazier and DeBusschere kept other teams honest. Frazier averaged 20.9 points per game, and DeBusschere's 10 rebounds per game were second only to Reed's 13.9 boards. Up to 1970, New York, which had been in the NBA since 1946, had never made it to the finals. The Knicks started the 1969–70 season as strong as they ended it. They won 14 of their first 15 games en route to a franchise-best 60–22 record. Later in the season, the Knicks ran off a then-record 18-game winning streak. Reed averaged 21.7 points per game and was voted MVP of the regular season and of the NBA All-Star Game. The Knicks ended the regular season with the best record, but they were not yet champions.

Reed Stands Tall, Plays Tall

New York was favored to win the NBA championship, but the Knicks were hardly expecting a cakewalk. In the first round of the playoffs, they faced their East Coast rivals from Baltimore. After splitting the first four games, Reed gave one of the most dominating performances of his career in game five, scoring 36 points and grabbing 36 rebounds in a 101–80 win at Madison Square Garden. The Bullets evened the series in game six, but New York cruised to the semifinals with a 127–114 win in game seven. Next, the Knicks dispatched the Milwaukee Bucks in five games to advance to their first final where they faced the Los Angeles Lakers, who boasted a roster that featured future Hall of Famers Wilt Chamberlain, Jerry West and Elgin Baylor.

Reed's heroics in game seven overshadowed what was already one of the most exciting NBA finals in league history. The Knicks won the series opener at the Garden as Reed led all scorers with 37 points in a 124–112 win. The Knicks, like the rest of the teams in the league, were unable to stop guard Jerry West, who scored 34 points as the Lakers squeaked by with a 105–103 win in game two, and the teams headed to Los Angeles. Both game three and game four went into overtime, with each team winning one contest.

The Knicks especially proved their mettle in game three. Keith Erickson's 40-foot shot at the buzzer gave the Lakers a 56–42 halftime lead. But New York battled back and took a 102–100 lead when Dave DeBusschere hit a 15-foot jumper with five seconds left in regulation. Chamberlain then inbounded to West, who dribbled forward three steps and fired a shot and scored from 63 feet away to send the game into overtime. But West missed all five of his shots in the extended period, and the Knicks won 111–108. Reed was the game's high scorer with 38 points.

After the Lakers evened the series at two games apiece, the teams headed back east for game five. Los Angeles jumped to an early 25–15 lead in the first quarter when Reed strained two muscles in his right thigh driving for a layup. The Knicks captain fell to the court in pain. He limped off the floor and did not return. Walt Frazier led the comeback with 21 points, and sub Cazzie Russell added 20 as New York rallied for a 107–100 win. Ahead now 3–2 in the best-of-seven series, the Knicks returned to

Los Angeles to try to win their first championship. They needed another total team effort like in game five, since Reed would not be able to play. What happened in LA left the team numb—Chamberlain scored 45 points and West added 33 as the Lakers cruised to a 135–122 win in game six.

A Moment in Time

The big question, in fact the only question, that people were asking before game seven of the 1970 NBA finals wasn't, "Can the Knicks win?"—it was, "Can Willis play?" That's because the former proposition was all but impossible without the latter. Reed was the only player missing from the floor when the teams began their pre-game warm up before the scheduled 8:00 PM tipoff. At 7:34 PM, the crowd seated directly across from the Knicks locker room stood up as a giant shadow began to come toward them. Section by section rose like a wave and started to cheer as Reed walked out onto the court. His teammates, as well as the Lakers, paused as he picked up a ball. The crowd in the famed arena then erupted when the team's captain hit his first practice shot.

A sense of relief filled the crowd, and the confidence among the Knicks soared. "It was like having your left arm sewn back on," said teammate Cazzie Russell. The Lakers won possession on the opening tipoff, but it was all downhill for them from there. After LA missed its initial shot, the Knicks came down the floor with their injured but able center trailing. Walt Frazier hit an open Reed, who nailed a jumper from the top of the key. He scored again on the Knicks' next possession and spent the rest of the first half harassing Chamberlain, who only made two-of-nine shots against his injured foe. By the time Reed left the game late in the second quarter, the Knicks led 61–37 and cruised to a 113–99 win, capturing their first NBA championship. In the end, Reed finished with just four points, but Frazier stepped up his game and led all scorers with 36; Dick Barnett also had 21, and Dave DeBusschere and Bill Bradley added 18 and 17 respectively.

There was high drama before the game, but certainly not in selecting a MVP for the NBA finals—Reed was the unanimous choice. Reed's heroics provided the most dramatic moment in what was the team's, as well as his own, greatest season. Reed was the first player in league history to win the MVP award for the regular season, the All-Star game and the playoffs.

No Reed, No Championship

Although the nucleus of the Knicks' first championship team remained intact the next year, they fell short of their quest to repeat with a heartbreaking loss in the first round of the playoffs to their old nemesis, the Baltimore Bullets. Willis Reed missed all but 11 games in 1971–72, but the Knicks still advanced to the NBA finals. The acquisitions of quality veterans Jerry Lucas and Earl "The Pearl" Monroe provided the much-needed help with scoring and on defense. Guard Walt Frazier led the team in scoring with 23.2 points per game while Dick Barnett and Monroe averaged a total of 23 points per game as they split time on the other half of the backcourt. The 6-foot-8 Lucas had an excellent jumper and was a solid rebounder, but he was brought to New York to complement Reed, not replace him. New York finished second in the East behind Boston (56–26)—their 48–34 record was their worst in four years.

The Knicks beat Baltimore and Boston to advance to the finals, where they once again faced Los Angeles, who, at 69–13, had the best record in the NBA. Without their captain, however, the Knicks fell in five games.

One-Year Wonders No More

The New York Knicks who were guided by coach Red Holzman to three NBA finals and two championships from 1970 to 1973 were not a great team. They were a good team, a solid team, a fine team, a smart team, but also a team filled with players who were not shy about stepping up and performing in the clutch. Sure, they needed Willis Reed to win, but what were the Celtics without Larry Bird, or the Bulls without Michael Jordan? Reed returned and played in 69 games in 1972–73, but he was clearly no longer the dominant player he had once been. Now, he averaged less than 30 minutes per game. Once one of the NBA's dominating big men, Reed's scoring and rebound totals fell from a high of 21 points per game and 13 boards in 1969–70 to 11 points per game and 8 boards in 1972–73.

In 1969–70, his teammates were supporting players; this time, the 1972–73 team was truly an ensemble cast. They improved to 57–25 but again finished a distant second to Boston, who led the NBA with a regular-season record of 68–14. The Knicks dispatched Baltimore and Boston in the playoffs and met the LA Lakers in the NBA finals for the third time in four years. Unlike their previous bouts, New York won with defense. Reed and Lucas tag-teamed Chamberlain, causing the Lakers center fits throughout the finals, where a year earlier Lucas was incapable of stopping "Wilt the Stilt" by himself. Picking his spots, Reed averaged 16 points and nine rebounds for the series. But by neutralizing Chamberlain, the Knicks won in five games, and once again, Reed was voted MVP of the playoffs.

With the final buzzer, the game and an era had passed. The cast that led their respective teams in those three head-to-head showdowns never played in another NBA final. Yet 10 players—Reed, DeBusschere, Bradley, Frazier, Monroe and Lucas, along with their Lakers counterparts Chamberlain, Jerry West, Elgin Baylor and Gail Goodrich—earned enshrinement in the Naismith Memorial Basketball Hall of Fame.

New York Nets

Barry Makes Nets Contenders

Like Reggie Jackson in 1978, when Rick Barry arrived on Long Island to play for the Nets, he brought his star with him. One of the best pure shooters in the history of basketball, the 6-foot-7, 210-pound small forward is the only player to lead the NCAA, NBA and ABA in scoring. The Roselle Park, New Jersey, native was an All-American at the University of Miami and led the nation in scoring in his senior season (37.4 points per game) in 1964–65. Barry was a first-round pick of the San Francisco Warriors in 1965 and led the NBA in scoring his second season with 35.6 points per game. He then jumped to the Oakland Oaks of the upstart American Basketball Association (ABA) but had to sit out a season before joining the team. He returned to the court for the 1968–69 season but played in just 35 games because of a knee injury. Yet, his 35.0 average was again a league high.

Barry was soon traded to the Washington Capitols, who became the Virginia Squires, but after one season in D.C., he wanted out and was traded to the New York Nets before the 1970–71 season. In his two seasons with New York, the team actually played their games on Long Island; the eventual 12-time All-Star led the Nets to the playoffs both times, averaging 29.4 and 31.5, respectively. In his second and last season with the Nets, they advanced to the ABA finals, where they lost to the Indiana Pacers 4–2.

With Barry and a supporting cast that included center Billy Paultz, Nets fans were looking forward to the future. Unfortunately, Barry had signed a futures contract with his old team, the Warriors, before arriving in New York. He went to law court in an attempt to void the deal and remain with the Nets, but the court ruled that Barry must honor the contract, and his days with the Nets came to an end. Although he played just four seasons in the ABA, he had the highest scoring average (30.5) in the league's 10-year run.

Besides his prolific scoring ability, Barry drew attention for his unique approach to foul shooting. He'd grab the ball at the sides with each of his hands, then slightly squatting, would toss the ball under-handed toward the hoop. Although many people were baffled at Barry's technique, his success at the line should have won some converts. Seven times he led the NBA or ABA in free-throw shooting percentage and never finished lower than third in that category. Barry, who retired as the best free-throw shooter in history, was elected into the Hall of Fame in 1987.

Knicks Destroy Nets

New York sports fans and the media have cursed the owners of the Dodgers and Giants as avarice scum for fleeing for greener pastures on the West Coast. Yet they gave a pass to a New York sports franchise that squeezed another local team into near bankruptcy and eventual demise 35 years ago. The New York Nets were a solid team that had the most exciting and talented player in professional basketball, Julius Erving. With "Dr. J" leading the way, the Nets won two of the last three ABA league titles before the league merged with the NBA in 1976.

To further enhance the team's prospects when they began play in the NBA, Nets owner Roe Boe traded for Nate "Tiny" Archibald, a top guard and perennial All-Star. Coach Kevin Loughery was confident of his team's chances of competing against the NBA's best. The Nets had to pay a $3-million entry fee to join the more established league. Then the NBA and the Knicks decided to enforce their "territorial claims" to the New York metropolitan area and demanded $4.8 million more from the Nets. Boe also had to re-sign his top player Erving, but there was no way that he could afford to give Erving a new contract as well as make the payments to the NBA and the Knicks.

George Steinbrenner's group purchased the Yankees in 1973 for $10 million and the Joan Payson estate sold the Mets in 1980 for $20 million. So what could the Nets have been worth in 1976? Boe decided to sell Erving to Philadelphia just to cover his NBA entry fee. But things just kept getting worse for the Nets when Archibald broke his ankle early in the season. It was the first of five consecutive losing seasons for the Nets, who relocated to New Jersey after the 1976–77 campaign. Meanwhile, Erving helped turn the 76ers into a championship team.

Nets fans are left to wonder how much better the franchise could have been if fate had acted in their favor. Two years before Erving arrived in a trade, they lost the services of scoring-machine Rick Barry when a futures contract he had signed with the Golden State Warriors was enforced by a federal judge. A team that featured future Hall of Famers Barry, Erving and Archibald would have struck fear into opposing teams—especially the Knicks.

Chapter Six

Kings of the Ring

Dempsey's Becomes a Landmark

After he won the heavyweight boxing title in 1919, Jack Dempsey spent most of his time living and boxing in New York City. It was the "Golden Age of Sports," and Dempsey—not Babe Ruth—was the biggest star of the sports world. Before Dempsey became champ, heavyweight title fights took place in hastily put together outdoor arenas. Dempsey didn't just sell out Madison Square Garden, but crowds of more than 80,000 jammed the Polo Grounds and Yankee Stadium to see "Jack the Giant Killer" destroy his opponents. He was responsible for the sport's first $1-million gate when he defeated Georges Carpentier in 1921, and more than 100,000 people paid to attend both of his fights with Gene Tunney.

To appreciate Dempsey's star power, just consider that at a time when Babe Ruth was baseball's highest paid player earning $80,000 per year, Dempsey earned more than 15 times what Babe earned. From 1926 to 1927, the "Manassa Mauler's" ring earnings for three fights totaled more than

$1.3 million: Tunney I ($700,000), Jack Sharkey ($250,000) and Tunney II ($400,000). And in his spare time, Dempsey earned $1300 per week as the lead of a play on Broadway.

By the time he retired, the Manassa Mauler had become a full-time New Yorker. In 1935, he opened Jack Dempsey's Restaurant, first at the corner of 50th Street across Eighth Avenue from the old Madison Square Garden, and later at 1619 Broadway, where his partner was Jack Amiel, whose colt, Count Turf, won the Kentucky Derby. Dempsey's was not only popular with sports fans but also with patrons of the theater and tourists from around the world. The former champ was an active owner who greeted customers on a daily basis, and he eventually became one of the Big Apple's iconic figures.

Dempsey's restaurant became so famous that it was used as a go-to backdrop for movies that were filmed in New York. In the first *Godfather* movie, when Al Pacino's character, Michael Corleone, goes to meet the two men he believes are responsible for trying to kill his father, he's told that they'll pick him up outside of Jack Dempsey's. The restaurant's neon marquee is clearly visible in the film. Unfortunately, in 1973 the landlord decided not to renew the lease, and Dempsey's closed after 28 years of service.

The man whose parents moved from West Virginia to Colorado in 1880 in a covered wagon died in 1983 at 87. Dempsey left home in his early teens and rode the rails from town to town, earning money fighting miners and lumberjacks in bouts staged in saloons.

He grew up in what was still the Wild West and became one of the top sports idols during the Roaring Twenties. With him, the link to the Golden Age of Sports and to America's untamed frontier had passed—he was the first one of the giants of his era to arrive, and the last to leave. Sports historian Bert Randolph Sugar put it best when he said, "Dempsey put the roar in the Roaring Twenties."

Homicide Hank Earns His Reputation

The 1920s and '30s were a time when notorious gangsters were considered quasi-celebrities, making headlines as they robbed banks and committed murder while evading law enforcement officials. Men like Al "Scarface" Capone, "Machinegun" Kelly and "Baby Face" Nelson all made the Most Wanted list. But when journalists wrote about the exploits of "Homicide Hank," they weren't talking about a criminal but one of the most exciting and successful boxing champions in history.

Henry Armstrong was born in 1912 in Columbus, Mississippi, but grew up in St. Louis. He turned pro in 1931 at 18, fighting mostly in California and other West Coast venues. He pulverized opponents with a non-stop attack and rained punches at a rate that would have impressed even Machinegun Kelly. Armstrong, who some also dubbed "Hurricane Hank," opened 1937 with 22 consecutive wins, all but one inside the distance, and earned a world title shot against featherweight champion Petey Sarron on October 29 at Madison Square Garden. Armstrong dominated the fight from the opening bell and Sarron fell in round six. The new champ struggled to make the 126-pound weight limit and knew his future lay at higher weights.

After winning the featherweight title, Armstrong won 14 consecutive non-title fights above the weight against top contenders below 150 pounds. He caught the attention of welterweight champion Barney Ross, who agreed to put his 147-pound crown on the line on May 31, 1938, at the Madison Square Garden Bowl, an outdoor facility in Queens. Armstrong, who weighed 133 pounds for the fight, dominated Ross, who was a two-division champ himself, and earned a lopsided unanimous decision. Armstrong was now the reigning champion in two divisions.

Since he was able to make the lightweight class limit of 135 pounds, Armstrong's managers targeted Lew Ambers, who happened to be the world champion at that weight. Ambers, who hailed from Herkimer, a tiny village north of Syracuse, was no match for Armstrong when they met at Madison Square Garden on August 17. Despite being penalized four times for low blows, Armstrong won a unanimous decision over 15 rounds. In less than a year, he won world titles at 126, 147 and 135 pounds. No other boxer had ever accomplished such a feat.

Sugar Sours in the Heat

In the summer of 1952, middleweight champion "Sugar" Ray Robinson was acknowledged as the best boxer in the world, pound for pound. At 5-foot-11,

157 pounds, the 31-year-old Robinson had excellent hand and foot speed and a sturdy chin; not to mention, he possessed one-punch knockout power with either hand, and he was perhaps the most graceful and skilled boxer to ever set foot in the squared circle.

Robinson, who had earlier won the world welterweight title, boasted a record of 131–2–2, and he avenged both losses by scoring prohibitive victories in the rematches. No one was surprised that Sugar Ray was a betting favorite when he stepped into the ring to challenge world light heavyweight champion Joey Maxim on June 25 at Yankee Stadium.

The fight had originally been scheduled for June 23, but torrential rains forced a two-day postponement. New York was in the midst of a heat wave at the time, but it was decided that the fight would still take place. Robinson was in perfect condition, though he spotted Maxim a 16-pound advantage.

The temperature was 103°F when the fight began, and that didn't even include the heat being generated from the lights above the ring. Robinson took an early lead, landing punches with ease and skillfully avoiding whatever offense Maxim tried to muster. Neither fighter was aware that fans in attendance were leaving because of the suffocating conditions. Eventually, referee Ruby Goldstein threw in the towel following round 10 and was replaced by Ray Miller.

Meanwhile, Robinson's punches were losing their snap, but he was far ahead on points. Maxim appeared the fresher of the two, but he was unable to seize control of the bout. Robinson's legs grew increasingly wobbly during round 13, and Maxim took advantage and landed a few blows. At the bell, Sugar Ray clung to the ropes as he walked to a corner—but it wasn't *his* corner. Robinson's trainers rushed over to grab the disoriented boxer and quickly led him back to his stool for a much-needed rest. But when the bell sounded again for round 14, Robinson was unable to continue. Maxim was awarded a technical knockout. The three judges' scorecards later revealed that Sugar Ray was ahead 10–3, 9–3–1 and 7–3–3.

A Meetin' of Unbeatens

You'd be hard-pressed to find two personalities more different than Joe Frazier and Muhammad Ali. Frazier was the son of a poor sharecropper from South Carolina. Like most boxers at of that time, he was respectful of his opponents, and while confident, "Smokin' Joe" didn't brag. Frazier, who had moved to Philadelphia as a teenager, attacked his opponents with reckless abandon and constant pressure. Ali, on the other hand, had an abundance of charm and charisma. He was boastful, usually in a humorous manner, but could be mean-spirited and controversial. In the ring, however, the "Louisville Lip" backed up his bragging with spectacular victories. He was as fast as he was flashy. The circumstances that brought the two boxers together on March 8, 1971, made it one of the most anticipated sporting events of the 20th century.

Known as Cassius Clay at the time, Ali had won the heavyweight title from Sonny Liston in 1964. Shortly after beating Liston, the new champion announced that he had converted from Christianity to Islam and had joined a Chicago-based, hate-mongering sect known as the Nation of Islam. Now known as Muhammad Ali, he incurred further wrath from the media and public by refusing induction into the U.S. Army during the Vietnam War. He was convicted of draft evasion in 1967 and sentenced to five years in federal prison. He was immediately stripped of the heavyweight title. Unlike Dempsey, who was acquitted of draft evasion after a speedy trial in 1920, Ali's appeals took several years (his conviction was eventually overturned by the U.S. Supreme Court in June 1971).

Ali's exile from boxing lasted from the spring of 1967 until September 1970. During that time, Frazier, a gold medalist at the 1964 Olympics, had turned pro and steadily climbed the heavyweight rankings. In March 1968, he beat Buster Mathis for the New York state version of the heavyweight title and unified the championship with a fifth-round knockout of World Boxing Association champion Jimmy Ellis at Madison Square Garden. Frazier sympathized with Ali's predicament and, knowing that a showdown with the former champ would provide him with a lucrative payday, spoke to boxing authorities and state commissions on the former champ's behalf. Ali was granted a boxing license again in 1970 and knocked out top contenders Jerry

Quarry (in three rounds) and then Oscar Bonavena (in 15 rounds) to set up the showdown with Frazier.

In promoting the fight, Ali's antics infuriated Frazier. The boasting and bragging was one thing, but when Ali cast Frazier as a "champion of the establishment"—and some used the more pejorative term "white man's champ"—it was as repugnant as it was uncalled for. But for many, the statement rang true. All in all, this was going to be a boxing match that transcended sports.

It seemed like everyone had an opinion. To Ali, the fight was a chance to get back what was unjustly taken from him. It was an opportunity to strike a blow against all the people who had criticized him on a variety of issues: race, religion and the war in Vietman, not to mention his sometimes-obnoxious personality. To Frazier, it was a chance to erase any doubt from the minds of sports fans who still considered Ali the champ. On a very personal level, Frazier didn't just want to defeat Ali; he wanted to inflict a beating on him because of the personal insults and the effects the taunting had on his children.

The sold-out crowd at Madison Square Garden on March 8 was so full of celebrities that ringside announcer Johnny Addie, who would normally have introduced a few of the non-boxers, started to drop a few names, then abruptly stopped. "Celebrities in the crowd tonight include…everyone, here is a celebrity—hello, Frank (Sinatra)."

The 6-foot-3, 215-pound former champion was 31–0 with 18 knockouts, while the 5-foot-11, 205-pound Frazier was 26–0 with 23 inside the distance. At the opening bell, the two fighters—who each earned a record $2.5 million for the fight—sprang from their corners and gave the Garden crowd and the millions watching around the world in theaters and sports arenas an action-packed 15-round spectacular.

Ali landed more hits, with flashier punches and combinations, while Frazier bored in on his adversary with a crippling body attack supplemented by left hooks to the jaw. The outcome seemed in the balance until round 15, when Frazier landed a thundering left hook to Ali's jaw that dropped the former champ for a count of four. Frazier earned a unanimous decision.

Champ Loses Crown and Family Jewels

Lightweight champion Ken Buchanan entered the ring at Madison Square Garden on the night of June 26, 1972, expecting a tough defense of his World Boxing Association title that he was putting on the line against Roberto Duran of Panama. The Scotsman was aware of his challenger's aggressive reputation. Nine months earlier at the Garden, Duran scored a crushing first-round knockout of local favorite Benny Huertas on the undercard of Buchanan's defense against Ismael Laguna. The performance impressed the fans and media, who flooded the champ with questions about his future opponent.

Duran sprang from his corner at the opening bell and attacked Buchanan, scoring a knockdown in the first minute of the fight. The champ got up and regrouped, and the two waged a spirited fight for the next 13 rounds. Buchanan, one of the best pure boxers of his era, complained to the referee about Duran's roughhouse tactics, and on several occasions the two men exchanged punches after the bell. The pace intensified in round 13 as the champion gallantly tried to retain the title that seemed to be slipping with each passing round.

As the bell sounded to end the round, the boxers once again continued to throw punches—then, just as referee Johnny LoBianco stepped between the two combatants, Duran nailed Buchanan in the groin. The champ grimaced in pain as he slumped to the canvas. Like most men who've taken a hard shot to the family jewels, Buchanan needed a lot more than the one-minute interval between rounds to recover. With Buchanan unable to continue, Duran was awarded a 13th-round TKO victory and the world title.

Jewels on the Line

Roberto Duran and Ken Buchanan were lightweights, but on three other occasions, a boxer's family jewels have come under assault in a major heavyweight bout. After Jack Dempsey lost his world title to Gene Tunney in 1926, he needed to win a tune-up in order to get a rematch. Dempsey had all he could handle when he faced top contender Jack Sharkey on July 21, 1927, at Yankee Stadium. Sharkey, a superior boxer, was giving the former champ fits. Dempsey's only hope was making the boxing match more of a brawl as he used his elbows, shoulders and an occasional low blow to rough up Sharkey. After the fighters broke following a spirited exchange in round seven, Dempsey landed a borderline punch to Sharkey's midsection. Sharkey grimaced and turned to complain to the referee. Dempsey then stepped in and threw a perfect left hook to Sharkey's jaw. Sharkey fell to the canvas and the referee first paused and then counted Sharkey out.

Four years later, Sharkey challenged German Max Schmeling for the heavyweight title that was vacated when Gene Tunney retired in 1929. In the second round, Sharkey threw a punch that landed below the belt and dropped Schmeling to the canvas. The German's cornermen motioned for him to stay down and complained to the referee that their boxer could not continue. The referee agreed and Sharkey was disqualified. Schmeling became the only boxer to win the heavyweight crown on a foul.

Sixty-six years passed before another heavyweight's family jewels were assaulted in such a manner in a New York boxing ring. Perhaps former champion Riddick Bowe of Brooklyn should have been prepared for such an assault when he faced Andrew Golota on July 11, 1996, at Madison Square Garden. After all, Golota, who had immigrated to Chicago from Krakow, Poland, had established a reputation as one of the roughest and dirtiest fighters of his era, being dubbed the "Foul Pole."

Golota dominated Bowe from the outset, landing the cleaner, harder, legal blows. But he also waged an assault below the belt that shocked the crowd,

Bowe (of course) and the referee, who warned Golota several times before penalizing him on three separate occasions. Golota was still slightly ahead on points when he felled Bowe again in the seventh round and was finally disqualified. The two met again in a rematch in December in Atlantic City. Once again, the Foul Pole dominated the action just as he had at the Garden. Despite being penalized for low blows, Golota was ahead on the judges' scorecards when he was disqualified for repeated low blows in the ninth round.

The Big Men of the Big Apple

The Big Apple boasts four men who have won the title of undisputed heavyweight champion of the world. Their reigns spanned 80 years, and they were as different as the eras they lived in. The first, and best, was Gene Tunney, an excellent scientific boxer who won the title from Jack Dempsey in 1926. He was followed by Floyd Patterson, another superb boxer who would have fared even better had he been born in an earlier era when heavyweights weighed less than 200 pounds. Mike Tyson and Riddick Bowe won their titles and made headlines from the mid-1980s through the '90s. Although both men displayed flashes of brilliance, their criminal acts and other unsavorily behavior listed on their rap sheets eventually surpassed, in quality and quantity, anything they ever accomplished in the ring.

The Matador

Gene Tunney was one of the great scientific boxers of his era. Born to Irish immigrants in 1898, he was the only one of the Big Apple's four heavyweight champs born and raised in Manhattan; the other three were from Brooklyn.

Tunney won the U.S. Expeditionary Forces light heavyweight title during World War I and turned pro when he was honorably discharged upon his return home after the Armistice was signed. Known as the "Fighting Marine," Tunney had the chiseled good looks of an action hero, but he could mix it up with the toughest boxers of his time. From 1922 to 1925, he waged an epic five-bout series with Hall of Famer Harry Greb, the only man to ever defeat him. It was Tunney's two fights with Jack Dempsey, however, that cemented his place in boxing history.

The first fight took place on September 23, 1926, in Philadelphia before a record crowd of 120,000. Employing a disciplined game plan, Tunney tamed and out-boxed the Manassa Mauler, who had spent eight years attacking and then beating challengers into submission, and won a unanimous decision over 10 rounds. Dempsey's only display of offense in their two fights came in their historic September 22, 1927, rematch at Soldier in Chicago. Dempsey dropped Tunney with a combination in the seventh round. But the ex-champion failed to go to a neutral corner as the rules dictated—the referee could not begin his count until Dempsey complied. The extra time allowed Tunney to clear his head. He survived the round and cruised to a unanimous decision. He then won a unanimous decision over Tom Heeney in his next title defense in 1928. He retired, as champion, with a record of 81–1–3 with 48 knockouts.

The Youngest and First Two-time Champ

Floyd Patterson was undersized as heavyweights go, but he had an oversized heart. The two-time New York Golden Gloves champion won a gold medal at the 1952 Olympics in Helsinki as a middle-weight when he was just 17 years old. He turned pro under the tutelage of trainer Cus D'Amato, who maneuvered his young charge into a shot at the heavyweight title that was vacated when Rocky Marciano retired. He won the world title on November 30, 1956, when he stopped light heavy-weight champ Archie Moore in the fifth round in Chicago to become, at 21 years 10 months old, the youngest heavyweight champion in history.

Patterson made four successful defenses before losing the title to Ingemar Johnsson of Sweden via a third-round knockout on June 26, 1959, at Yankee Stadium. A year later at the Polo Grounds, Patterson knocked out the Swede to become the first man to win back the title. Patterson eventually lost the title to Sonny Liston in 1961, but he didn't retire until 1972 with a final record of 55–8–1 with 50 knockouts. Known as one of the true gentlemen of the sport, he died in 2006 at age 71.

Chapter Seven

New Yorkers Make Global Impact

Legendary Gridiron Pioneer and Coach

Few men have had as big an impact on their sport as Glen Scobey Warner. The future gridiron coaching giant was born in 1871 in Springville, about 30 miles south of Buffalo. He captained and starred on Cornell's football team, where he was hung with the moniker "Pop" because he was the oldest player on the team. After graduation in 1902, Warner returned home and became a lawyer. A few months later, he turned his back on the law and accepted a job as an assistant football coach at Iowa State. In 1895, he got his first head-coaching gig at the University of Georgia, and over the next 43 years, he became one of the game's great innovators and most successful coaches in college football history.

His tenure at the University of Pittsburgh (1915–23) saw his Panthers team win three National Championships (1915, 1916 and 1918) and at one point won 33 consecutive games during that span. He then moved on to Stanford, where the 1924 edition of the Cardinal went 7–0–1 during the regular season and went to the Rose Bowl, where they met undefeated Notre Dame, which was coached by Knute Rockne and powered by the famed "Four Horsemen." On New Year's Day in 1926, Stanford proved no match for the Fighting Irish and lost 27–10.

Warner's 1926 and 1927 teams won the Pacific Coast Conference, going 10–0–1 and 8–2–1, respectively, and appeared in the Rose Bowl both seasons. They battled Alabama to a 7–7 tie on New Year's Day in 1927 and won recognition as national champions, the fourth time a Warner-coached team won the honor. A year and a day later, Stanford edged Pitt 7–6 in the Rose Bowl for Pop's only win in the "Granddaddy of Them All."

It was during the second of his two stints at the Carlisle, Pennsylvania, Indian School, where he "coached" Jim Thorpe in track and football, that Warner is most remembered for. Thorpe, who was a member of the Sac-and-Fox Indian tribe, was already a sensation in track, but the Oklahoma native had to pester a reluctant Warner into giving him a tryout on the gridiron. Warner once remarked of his naturally gifted star player, "Thorpe rarely gave more than 50 or 60 percent of himself. But when he went all out—well, it was humanly impossible for anyone to be better." Thorpe, who is generally regarded as the greatest athlete in American history, went on to win two gold medals, in the pentathlon and decathlon, at the 1912 Olympics. He also played six years of Major

League Baseball and became one of the founders and best players of the NFL.

Football historians credit Warner for several innovations, including the three-point stance, shoulder and thigh pads, the spiral punt, the screen pass, the single-wing and double-wing formations, numbering on players' jerseys and improved helmets. He also introduced blocking sleds and tackling dummies to practice routines. All six schools that Pop led had winning records: Georgia (7–4), Carlisle (114–42–8), Cornell (36–13–3), Pittsburgh (60–12–4), Stanford (71–17–8) and Temple (31–18–9). Warner—who retired after the 1938 season at Temple as the all-time winningest coach with a career mark of 319–106–32—currently ranks seventh in career wins.

Olympic Champ Led a Novel Life

Young Ed Eagan of Denver was like most boys of his generation who grew up in the early part of the 20th century. Eagan, born on April 26, 1897, immersed himself in dime-store novels and serial adventures of heroic figures from bygone ages as well as some contemporary figures. This escape into reading was particularly important in Eagan's case because his father died in a train accident when Ed was a child; he and his siblings were raised under humble conditions by a single mother.

It was a blessing for Mrs. Eagan that her son chose Frank Merriwell as his idol. Merriwell was an upstanding hero and the main character of author

Gilbert Patten's best-selling novels. Patten, who published the series in *Tip Top Weekly* under the pseudonym Burt L. Standish, created a character that many boys could dream about but very few could actually emulate with any degree of success. After a youth spent at prestigious boarding schools, the Yale-educated Merriwell became an elite athlete of unmatched versatility. He always came through in the clutch and he exemplified good sportsmanship. Off the field, he was the epitome of a refined and educated gentleman.

Eagan became a model student and won a scholarship to the University of Denver and eventually earned a degree from Yale. He volunteered for military service during World War I, and as a member of the American Expeditionary Forces, won an interservice boxing championship. He eventually qualified for the 1920 Olympics in Antwerp, Belgium, and won a gold medal as a light heavyweight.

When Eagan returned to America after the Olympics, he enrolled in Harvard Law School. But that was put on hold when he was awarded a prestigious Rhodes Scholarship to Oxford University in England. Eagan completed his law degree and returned home to become a prosecutor in New York. He remained active in sports and helped Gene Tunney train for his upset of heavyweight champ Jack Dempsey in 1926. Eagan moved in elite circles and was a good friend of Jay O'Brien, the head of the U.S. Olympic Bobsled Committee. Just before the 1932 Olympics in Lake Placid, New York, a member of the four-man team had opted to compete in the two-man event, leaving his three teammates in a bind. And then unseasonably warm temperatures prevented the committee from holding formal Olympic trials. So, with time running short, O'Brien turned to his old friend for help.

Like his hero Merriwell, Eagan accepted the invitation to join the U.S. bobsled team, even though he had never even been in a bobsled before he arrived in Lake Placid. With Eagan on board, though, the U.S. team won gold. He became the first Olympian to win gold medals in different events at the summer and winter Olympics. Eagan then returned to his private life. He served as an assistant U.S. attorney for Southern New York and volunteered for the U.S. Army Air Corps during World War II. After the war, New York governors as well as President Eisenhower named Eagan to a few high-profile, sports-related posts, including Chairman of the New York State Athletic Commission, the president's People-to-People sports committee and director of sports programs for the 1964 World's Fair in New York. He remained a resident of Rye until his death in 1967 at age 69.

Four Golds and Four Records for Oerter

From the moment he first picked up an errant discus during track practice at Sewanhaka High School and casually threw it farther than anyone had every seen, Al Oerter left his teammates, opponents and track-and-field aficionados speechless. Oerter, who was born in Queens in 1936 and raised in Floral Park on Long Island, went out for the school's track team as a runner. But after witnessing his casual toss during practice, he left the track and achieved lasting world fame on the field inside the oval. He set a national high school record of 184 feet, 2 inches throwing the lighter discus used at the scholastic level. Oerter accepted a scholarship to the University of Kansas, where as a Jayhawk, he set a collegiate record and was a two-time national champion.

In his sophomore year, Oerter qualified for the 1956 Olympics in Melbourne, Australia. His appearance at those Games began a trek that would last four consecutive Olympiads, from 1956 to 1968. His Olympic odysseys had several similarities: each time, Oerter barely made the team and was not favored to win the event. And he not only won four gold medals, but he also beat the reigning world-record holder each time and set an Olympic record in the process. He arrived in Melbourne as the sixth-rated discus thrower in the world and won the event with a personal best of 184 feet, 10½ inches. His 194 feet, 2 inches bested the opposition at the 1960 Games in Rome. Then, four years later in Tokyo, he overcame torn rib cartilage and heaved the discus 200 feet, one inch, and he closed out his Olympic career in 1968 in Mexico City unleashing a career throw of 212 feet, 6 inches.

Oerter retired after the 1968 Games at age 32 with an impressive legacy that included an unprecedented four gold medals in the same event—long jumper Carl Lewis has since tied the feat—not to mention four world records and the distinction of being the first discus thrower to break 200 feet. When Oerter had graduated from Kansas in the late 1950s, amateur sports in the U.S. was just that—amateur. So he entered the business world and eventually became a computer analyst for Grumman Technologies, a leading defense and aerospace contractor located on Long Island. Oerter maintained his world-class status, but his training had to be done after putting in a nine-to-five work-day, and on the weekends.

The competitive bug never left him, however, and Oerter began training in the late 1970s in the hopes of earning a spot on the U.S. Olympic team and compet-ing at the 1980 Games in Moscow. In the year leading up to the Olympics, he threw 222 feet, 9 inches and 227 feet, 10½ inches. Both tosses would have been good enough to win gold in Moscow, but Oerter's best effort at the Olympic trials was 215 feet, 1 inch; he had to settle for fourth place. Many observers believed that had it not been for the U.S. boycott of the Moscow Games because of the Soviet Union's invasion of Afghanistan in 1979, Oerter probably would have risen to the occasion as he had so many times before and thrown the additional three feet he needed to place third and make the U.S. Olympic team for the fifth straight time. But because he knew he wouldn't be going to the Games, there was no incentive to put in his best effort.

His attempt to compete in the 1984 Olympic Games in Los Angeles also ended in disappointment when he suffered an injury at the trials. At age 47, Oerter finally retired from world competition, but he stayed active on the senior track-and-field circuit until his death in 2007.

Head West, Young Men

Big Apple baseball teams boast a who's-who of all-time great sports figures. Among this austere group are two founding fathers of another professional sports league. Jim Thorpe, who is regarded by many as the greatest athlete who ever lived, played six seasons of Major League Baseball, primarily with the Giants from 1913 to 1915 and 1917 to 1919. Thorpe was already one of the most famous athletes in the world even before he joined the big leagues. The Sac-and-Fox Native American gained fame as the star on Carlisle, Pennsylvania, Indian School's great football teams, and he won gold medals at the 1912 Olympics in the decathlon and pentathlon.

Like Thorpe, the switch-hitting George Halas also played his home games at the Polo Grounds but as a seldom-used outfielder for the Yankees in 1919. Halas had just two hits in 22 at-bats during his brief stay in New York. Both men, who enjoyed more success on the gridiron than on a baseball diamond, left baseball after the 1919 season and headed west. In 1920, Thorpe and Halas were among a group of seven men who met in Canton, Ohio, and founded the National Football League.

Volleyball Springs from Springfield, Massachusetts

When William Morgan ran away from home as a teenager, he dreamed of a life as a merchant seaman on the ships of the Erie Canal and Great Lakes. He never expected to be the inventor of a physical fitness alternative to basketball that would eventually become one of the most popular sports in the world.

Morgan, who was born in the Buffalo suburb of Lockport in 1870, quickly tired of the life of a merchant sailor. His parents sent him to the Mount Hermon School in Northfield, Massachusetts, where he graduated in 1891. While at school, he met James Naismith—the man who invented basketball in 1891—who urged him to attend the International YMCA Training School (now Springfield College) in Springfield, Massachusetts. Upon graduation in 1894, Morgan was again encouraged by Naismith to pursue a career as a physical fitness instructor. Morgan eventually became the physical education director at the YMCA in nearby Holyoke.

During his time at the Holyoke YMCA, Morgan determined that basketball was too strenuous for older gentlemen and he came up with an activity more suitable to their needs. By December 1895, he came up with a game in which two teams stood on opposite sides of a net that was 6 feet, 6 inches high, and team members would "volley" a ball to each other since the ball was not allowed to hit the ground. Morgan initially called the game "mintonette" because his new sport was related to badminton.

Originally there were no limits to the amount of players on a team, or how many times a ball could be hit before it went over the net. Over the next few months, Morgan's new game was fine-tuned—with those two aspects among the rules that were changed—and the game was introduced at Springfield College. Another important element was changed before the game's debut—its name. It now was called the more sensible "volley ball" (it did not become a single word until 1952).

Soon, volley ball was being played at many YMCAs across America. Perhaps the event that catapulted volley ball into an international game was the greatest historical event up to that time: World War I. Volley ball was introduced to troops of Allied countries by the American Expeditionary Troops in France, and the team aspect proved to be very popular with the soldiers. Morgan, however, left the field of physical fitness years before his invention became an international craze, yet he remained close with Springfield College and the volley ball community. Morgan left teaching in 1900 and eventually returned to Lockport and became a businessman. He lived there until his death in 1942, content in the knowledge that the game he invented brought a richer life to millions of people throughout the world. Volley ball was an exhibition sport at the 1924 Olympics in Paris. The sport's governing body, the Fédération Internationale de Volleyball, was formed in 1947, and volleyball finally became an Olympic sport for the 1964 Games in Tokyo. Beach volleyball was added to the Olympics in 1996.

Steelers Send Future Greats Packing

During the 1950s, the Pittsburgh Steelers held their summer football training camp at St. Bonaventure University, a small Catholic school in Olean, which is about four hours north of the Steel City by car. The Steelers had never won a playoff game and wouldn't until 1972. Perhaps the coaching staff's inability to recognize great talent was one of the reasons. During that decade, Jack Kemp—who was later an All-Pro and led the San Diego Chargers and Buffalo Bills to championships in the AFL—had a brief stint with Pittsburgh in 1957. The team's number-one draft pick that year, Len Dawson of Purdue, struggled through three seasons, completing just 6-of-17 passes he threw before he was traded to Cleveland.

Two years later, it appeared his career was over until he was signed by the Dallas Texans of the new AFL. Dawson led the Texans to an AFL championship in 1961, and later, when the team moved to Kansas City, he was the starting quarterback in Super Bowl I, a loss to Green Bay Packers, and Super Bowl IV, where he was MVP in the Chiefs' 24–7 win over the Minnesota Vikings. The inability of the Steelers coaches to either cultivate or support these two future great signal callers was bad enough and spoke to the franchise's futility.

But since these types of things usually happen in threes, the third quarterback that Pittsburgh sent packing never made the team's final roster but did eventually catch on with another team and have a Hall of Fame career. The team's 1955 ninth-round draft pick out of the University of Louisville was listed so far down the depth chart that he seldom got to take snaps in scrimmages that summer and spent most of his time playing catch with the owner's son on the vast open fields at St. Bonaventure. With a lack of opportunity to showcase his skills, John Constantine Unitas wasn't surprised to find himself sitting alone in the Olean bus station after he was cut from the team and wondering what he was going to do with the rest of his life.

He returned home and caught on with a semi-pro team and was eventually signed by the Baltimore Colts as a backup. By the end of the 1956 season, he was the starter. His next trip to New York came during the 1958 regular season against the Giants at Yankee Stadium. Although the Colts lost that encounter, they finished the season as the Western Division champs and returned to face the Giants with the NFL championship on the line. Unitas led the Colts to a thrilling 23–17 overtime victory over New York in a game that is considered one of the most significant in pro football history. Unitas led the Colts to two more NFL championships, appeared in two Super Bowls and set many passing records in his career.

Only Two Super Signal Callers

In the grand history of the Super Bowl, only two quarterbacks began their long road to the big game on the gridirons of the Empire State. Ron Jaworski was a three-sport star in high school in Lackawanna, a small suburb of Buffalo, and was drafted by the St. Louis Cardinals to play baseball. He opted instead for a football scholarship to Youngstown State, Ohio, where he starred in the early 1970s. He was drafted by the then–Los Angeles Rams. After a few seasons primarily as a backup, the "Polish Rifle" was traded to the Philadelphia Eagles. Under the tutelage of coach Dick Vermeil, Jaworski and the team improved every season until 1980, when they won the NFC East Division title and beat Dallas soundly, 20–7, to qualify for Super Bowl XV against Oakland in New Orleans.

Jaworski, now known by the moniker "Jaws," had his best season in 1980. He was voted to the Pro Bowl and garnered Player of the Year honors from several organizations. The season, however, ended on a sour note as Jaws was intercepted three times in a 27–10 loss to the Raiders. He remained with the Eagles through the 1986 season, but they never again contended for a championship. He spent the 1987 and 1988 seasons with Miami, then one with Kansas City before retiring from football. The final book on Jaws' 14-year pro career reads: 28,190 passing yards, 53.1 percent completion percentage and 179 touchdowns versus 164 interceptions.

Like Jaworski, Norman "Boomer" Esiason was a three-sport star in high school. The southpaw quarterback sensation led East Islip High School to an undefeated season his senior season and enjoyed a collegiate career at Maryland, where he set 17 school passing records. Drafted in the second round by Cincinnati in 1984, Esiason was starting by the end of his rookie year. He spent the next nine full seasons as the Bengals starter. The Long Island native made the Pro Bowl three times, including the team's Super Bowl season of 1988. Also like Jaworski, Esiason earned Player of the Year honors in his lone Super Bowl season, but the team was victimized by a last-minute, Joe Montana–led comeback in a 20–16 loss to San Francisco.

Esiason left the Queen City after the 1992 season and returned home to spend three seasons with the Jets, making the Pro Bowl in 1993, then spent one year in Arizona before returning to the Bengals for a curtain call in 1997. His final NFL stats read: 37,920 passing yards, 57 percent completion percentage and 247 touchdowns versus 184 interceptions.

Queen of the Waves

In 1974, a contrived tennis match between reigning women's tennis champion Billie Jean King and former men's champion Bobby Riggs was billed as "The Battle of the Sexes." The nation was riveted, but few should have been surprised when King, in her athletic prime, beat Riggs, who was a force on the men's tour—before World War II. Much was made of King's victory, yet the future tennis Hall of Famer nor her legion of supporters were clamoring for other matches against the top men's players of that time.

One wonders what Gertrude Ederle thought of the spectacle. Ederle was an Olympic champion swimmer at the 1924 Games in Paris and had set 29 world records in women's freestyle events from 100 to 800 meters during the 1920s. A year after she won one gold and two bronze medals at the Olympics, Ederle attempted to do something that only four people, all men, had ever accomplished: swim across the English Channel.

Before heading to England, Ederle garnered attention when she swam from Battery Park to Sandy Hook, New Jersey, a distance of more than 16 miles. Her route between France and England would be 21 miles if done in a straight line. Ederle first attempted the cross-channel ordeal in 1925 but was disqualified when one of her coaches, fearing she was drowning, jumped in the water to "save" her. Once Ederle was touched—she claimed she was just resting—she was disqualified, after covering 23 miles in eight hours, 43 minutes.

She spent the next year training and raising money through sponsorships for her second attempt to successfully navigate the treacherous waters between France and England. She entered the water at Cap Gris-Nez, France, on the morning of August 6, 1926. She could see a red ball on the shore, which was a warning to small boats that choppy waters posed a potential hazard. Smeared with sheep grease and accompanied by two tugboats filled with sponsors, coaches and two reporters, Ederle asked God for strength then waded into the water and began her aquatic journey to the land of Shakespeare. Along the way, she hummed the tune "Let Me Call You Sweetheart" to the rhythm of her stroke—how many times, she had no idea. This time, she gave her coaches strict instructions to not touch her until she walked ashore under her own power.

And 14 hours, 31 minutes later, she did. By completing the cross-channel crossing, Ederle not only became the first woman (fifth person ever), but she also bested the time of 16 hours, 33 minutes set by Enrique Tiraboschi of Argentina on August 13, 1923. Experts who accompanied her in the tugs estimated that with the currents and rough sea, Ederle actually swam approximately 35 miles. Perhaps the only person not entirely impressed with Ederle was a British immigration official who asked the exhausted American for her passport.

News of Ederle's record-setting swim spread quickly, and she received a hero's welcome when she returned to America a few weeks later. She was invited to the White House by President Coolidge, who called the swimmer "our best girl." Back home in New York, mayor Jimmy Walker gave Ederle a key to the city, and she became the first woman to have the honor of a ticker-tape parade down the "Canyon of Heroes."

In-depth Ederle

Gertrude Ederle, a daughter of a German immigrant, was born in Manhattan in 1905, one of seven children of Henry and Anna Ederle. She learned to swim during summers spent down on the Jersey Shore. A bout with measles as a child impaired her hearing, which was made worse by her swimming—doctors advised her to stay out of the water. But the woman who was dubbed "Queen of the Waves" felt more at home in the water. Her hearing was made worse by her two channel crossings, and eventually she went totally deaf.

In the years that followed, she toured with Vaudeville shows and did swimming exhibitions. A fall down a flight of stairs injured her spine, and she was bedridden in the 1930s. It was feared that she would never walk again. But with the same determination she showed in the waters between France and England, Ederle fully recuperated and took part in swimming exhibitions at the 1939 World's Fair, which was held in New York City. She enjoyed her time in the spotlight, which faded as time passed. Ederle became a swimming instructor for deaf children and lived modestly in Queens until she died in 2004 at age 98.

Queen "Mother" of the Waves

Gertrude Ederle's status as the only woman to swim the English Channel lasted just 22 days. While Ederle was basking in the glow of public adulation back home in America, Amelia Gade Corson entered the water at Cap Gris-Nez, France (the same place as Ederle) with two other swimmers, both men, to attempt her second crossing. Unlike Ederle, Corson was not a world-class athlete. The native of

Copenhagen, Denmark, was born in 1899 and started swimming as a child. She became an expert swimmer and started her own business as an instructor. Gade, as she was known before she was married, immigrated to America in 1919 and settled in New York City, where she taught swimming at a local YMCA as well as to navy recruits.

One of her first noteworthy accomplishments in the water occurred on June 26, 1921, when she swam around Manhattan Island, a 40-mile trip that took her 15 hours, 57 minutes. On September 8, 1921, she swam from Albany down the Hudson River to Battery Park in Manhattan. According to *The New York Times* coverage of the event, "Millie" covered approximately 153 miles on the swim, a distance of 143 miles in a straight line. Gade's elapsed time was six days, one hour and seven minutes. Although Gade stopped along the way, she never left the water. Her actual time swimming was 63 hours and 35 minutes.

That day, the fearless swimmer was accompanied by Clemington Corson, who shouted encouragement from a rowboat. The pair eventually married and had two children, who were age two and four when their mom made history in 1926. Though Cade lacked accomplishments in competitive swimming, she more than made up for it as a lifeguard; on three occasions, she was recognized by King Christian X of Denmark for saving lives. Shortly after arriving in New York, she received a Carnegie Medal of heroism for saving another swimmer.

Corson had attempted the channel crossing from England to France in 1923, but she was forced to concede to the elements after swimming 21 miles in 14 hours as a strong tide pulled her several miles off course when she was just two miles from the French coast. For her second attempt, one of Corson's sponsors, a New York businessman named L. Walter Lissberger, made a $5000 wager at 20-to-1 odds with Lloyds of London that Corson would make it across unaided. With her faithful companion accompanying her, the mother of two entered the water with two male hopefuls at 11:32 PM on August 28, 1926. Both men dropped out, but Corson battled the elements and walked ashore in England 15 hours, 29 minutes later. Although Corson failed to beat Ederle's record time, it was still faster than any man. Americans and New Yorkers toasted Corson upon her return. She was greeted by a large crowd when she arrived via ocean liner and was also given a ticker-tape parade.

Banach Brothers Bring Home Gold

Brothers Ed and Lou Banach were state wrestling champions at Port Jervis High School. Ed, who was born eight minutes before Lou, boasted a record of 97–8 and was New York state champ in 1977 and 1978. Lou was 65–2 and was state champion in 1977. Like their older brother Steve, the twins were offered scholarships to grapple for the University of Iowa, which at the time was the premier program in the nation. Led by coach Dan Gable, himself a scholastic champion in high school and NCAA champion at Iowa State and 1972 Olympic gold medalist, the Banachs joined a program that was in the midst of a record nine consecutive national titles (1978–85). As a Hawkeye, Ed's record was 141–9–1. He was an NCAA finalist four times and won three national titles. Lou was 90–14–2 and won two NCAA individual crowns (1981 and 1983). The pair then capped off their amateur careers by winning gold medals at the 1984 summer Olympics in Los Angeles; Lou at 220 pounds, and Ed at 198 pounds.

After a brief career as an assistant wrestling coach at Iowa State, Ed became an academic counselor at the university. After a stint in the army, Lou coached wrestling for a while at West Point and is currently a bank executive in Milwaukee. The eldest Banach brother, Steve, retired from the army in August 2010 after 27 years of service with a rank of lieutenant colonel.

Ordeal and Triumph

Louie Zamperini is not in any national sports Hall of Fame. And he never won an individual or team championship in college or professional sports. His story, because of his indomitable spirit and partly forged as a top high school miler and Olympic long distance runner, is one of triumph over insurmountable odds and should provide inspiration to us all.

Zamperini was born in Olean on January 26, 1917, to Italian immigrant parents but moved with his family to Torrance, California, when he was a child. He was a screw-up and a petty thief as a teenager, and only his older brother's intervention with the help of the authorities saved him from going to jail. His brother also encouraged him to go try out for the track team, which changed Louie's life forever. As a high school junior, Zamperini set a national scholastic record for the mile when he clocked four minutes, 21.2 seconds in 1935.

Knowing that he couldn't compete with world-class milers, Zamperini took advantage of a weak field and qualified for the U.S. Olympic team in the 5000 meters even though he'd only run the race three times. In Berlin, Zamperini qualified for the final event. He struggled and was in the middle of the pack for most of the race but decided to let it all hang out and clocked a 56-second final lap. He didn't win a medal, but his big kick was noticed by the 100,000 fans in the arena, who gave him a huge ovation. It also got the attention of none other than Adolf Hitler, who met Zamperini later that day and said, "You're the boy with the fast finish."

After returning home, Zamperini set his sights on the 1940 Olympics in Japan. But the Games were canceled with the onset of World War II. Zamperini joined the navy and was a crewman of a rescue squadron in the South Pacific. On a mission to search for a downed plane on May 27, 1943, the engine on Zamperini's plane failed and the plane crashed into the Pacific Ocean. Only Zamperini and two of the remaining 12 crewmen survived. They swam to one of the plane's life rafts, where they remained for the next 45 days. The three crewmen survived by killing and eating a few careless osprey that landed on the raft as well as the livers of small sharks that jumped into the raft.

On about the 30th day, one of the crewmen died, and the other two said a few prayers and lowered him into the water. Two weeks later, they came ashore on an island, but they were shocked to find out that it was inhabited by the Japanese Imperial Army. Zamperini and the other survivor spent the remaining two years in a Japanese POW camp. Whereas the survival rate for Allied POWS captured by Germans was 95 percent, of those soldiers, sailors, airmen and marines who surrendered to the Japanese, three out of five died in captivity.

Zamperini endured harsh treatment and torture at the hands of his captors, but he survived. When he returned home, he was haunted by his experiences as a POW as well as the harrowing ordeal at sea. He sought escape in alcohol to cope with his post-traumatic stress and began a downward spiral. Eventually, his wife, Cynthia, whom he married in 1946, urged him to attend a religious service featuring a young evangelist named Billy Graham. Zamperini was so moved by the experience that he was baptized and became a devout Christian and, like Graham, began preaching the gospel. He returned to Japan in 1950 and visited a prison that housed Japanese war criminals, some of whom were the same prison guards who had tortured him years earlier. They were shocked when Zamperini embraced them and forgave them for their treatment of him and the other prisoners. Zamperini continued to preach and travel and devoted much time to counseling at-risk youth. He is still alive, at age 94, and resides in California.

A Record Leap Still Stands

In July 1969, Neil Armstrong set foot on the moon and proclaimed, "That's one giant step for a man. One giant leap for mankind." While only a few astronauts were ever able to take leaps as significant as Armstrong, back on Earth, people were still talking about Bob Beamon's record-shattering leap in the long jump at the 1968 summer Olympics in Mexico City.

The Jamaica, Queens, native was born in 1947 and opted for athletics over joining a gang in the turbulent 1960s. He starred at Jamaica High School in basketball and track and won a scholarship to North Carolina A&T and later transferred to Texas–El Paso. Although Beamon set the world indoor record in the long jump (27 feet, 1 inch) on January 23 and then bested that mark with a record leap (27 feet, 2¾ inches) on March 15, he was not the favorite to win gold in Mexico City. The smart money was on the two long jumpers who were co–world record holders in the event: American Ralph Boston, the gold medalist from the Rome Games in 1960, and Igor Ter-Ovanesyan of the Soviet Union, both of whom leaped 27 feet, 4¾ inches.

Beamon, who fouled on his first two jumps at the Olympic trials, barely made the team. When he went to the line for his first jump, most of the 80,000 in the Olympic stadium were focused on the finals of the men's 400-meter dash. Boston and Ter-Ovanesyan hadn't even taken their warm-ups off. Beamon didn't notice anything different when he took off on his record-setting leap or when he pushed off with his right foot. In Mexico, the long jump was measured with an optical device that slid along a rail parallel to the landing pit. The device, however, proved useless because it was only 28 feet long. When Beamon returned to Earth, he had covered 29 feet, 2½ inches—a whopping 21¾ inches more than the current record. Track officials required a measuring tape to certify Beamon's jump. The two old record holders immediately knew that they'd be competing for no better than silver. In fact, East German Klaus Beer turned in the second-best jump (26 feet, 10 inches), while Boston (26 feet, 7 inches) took the bronze.

Beamon continued to jump and won a few other competitions, but he never again broke 27 feet. To put the magnitude of the jump into perspective, not even Carl Lewis—who won gold in 1984 and 1988 in the long jump—ever seriously challenged the record. Beamon's jump stood as a world record until 1991, when American Mike Powell leapt 29 feet, 4 inches at the world championships in Tokyo. Yet 44 years later, Beamon still holds the Olympic mark. His one big, giant leap may not have been one for mankind, but it was certainly one for the ages.

Chapter Eight

Gridiron Greats

New York Giants

The Ghost Saves the Franchise

Today, it's hard to believe that pro football struggled for more than 30 years to gain a permanent place in the conscience of sports fans. The NFL was five years old when local bookmaker Tim Mara was approached about buying into the league as the owner of its New York franchise. Mara figured that owning a New York franchise in *anything* was worth the $500 asking price. The Giants struggled on the field, with the aging Jim Thorpe as their main gate attraction. It took a "business arrangement" with Chicago Bears owner George Halas to keep the Big Apple entity afloat. Halas, one of the league's founders in 1920, had out-negotiated Mara for the services of the greatest college football player of the era, Red Grange of the University of Illinois. The "Galloping Ghost," as Grange was known, left college on a Thursday and was playing for the Bears within a week. Halas agreed to a hastily scheduled game against the Giants to help generate revenue for the New York team.

The arrangement paid off—for everyone involved—as a standing-room-only crowd of 70,000 jammed into the Polo Grounds on December 6, 1925, to see Grange return an interception for a touchdown in a Bears' 19–7 win. Grange, whose contract with the Bears called for a percentage of the gate, made approximately $40,000, while Mara, who was drowning in a sea of red ink, ended his inaugural season in the black. The New York Giants were now on sound financial footing.

Big Blue's Black Sheep

The Giants were soon among the NFL's elite franchises. They were one of the most successful on the field, and the Mara family ran the team with integrity. But that reputation was soiled in the days leading up to the 1946 NFL championship game when law enforcement authorities became aware that organized crime figures had contacted several New York players about throwing the title game scheduled for December 15 against the Bears at the Polo Grounds. The news media jumped on the story, and the day before the game, star quarterback Frank Filchock and running back Merle Hapes were interviewed by New York City mayor Bill O'Dwyer, NFL commissioner Bert Bell, police commissioner Arthur Wallander and Giants owner Tim Mara. Hapes admitted to being approached and was blocked from playing, while Filchock, who denied it, was allowed to play.

On the morning of the game, the district attorney's office announced that Filchock and Hapes had been offered $2500 each, plus the profits from a $1000 bet that Chicago would win by more than 10 points. The players also had been offered off-season jobs that were promised to bring them another $15,000.

Filchock was booed by the sellout crowd when he was introduced before the game, which the Giants lost 24–14. He played both ways and completed 9-of-26 passes for 126 yards and threw both Giants touchdowns in a contest that was tied 14–14 entering the fourth quarter. Even though Filchock also threw six interceptions on the day, it was determined that he gave an honest effort. Yet during the subsequent trial of the mobsters, four of whom were convicted, Filchock finally admitted he had also been contacted. The commissioner then banned both players indefinitely. After spending three seasons playing in the Canadian Football League, Filchock won reinstatement in the NFL but never again played pro football. Hapes, on the other hand, never played football again.

A Giant Who Stands Above Others

Jack Lummus never made All-Pro, never played on a championship team and never even scored a touchdown. In his only season with the Giants, he played end on the 1941 team that won the Eastern Division title with an 8–4 record but lost the NFL championship game in December to the Bears, 37–9. But like Chicago Bear Brian Piccolo, Lummus left a more important legacy for his heroics on a much bigger playing field. The Ellis County, Texas, native had been a two-sport star and attended Baylor University on an athletic scholarship. At Baylor, Lummus was an honorable mention All-America in football and earned All-Southwest Conference honors as a centerfielder.

He dropped out of Baylor in 1941 and played semi-pro baseball for a while, and then he signed up for the U.S. Army Air Corps but washed out of flight school after a minor accident. He then joined the NFL Giants for football that fall. After the nation went to war, Lummus joined the U.S. Marines in January 1942. He was an enlisted man but eventually graduated from Officers Candidate School and was commissioned a second lieutenant. By the autumn of 1944, he was with the 27th Marine Division and was preparing for the invasion of a little volcanic island called Iwo Jima. February 19, 1945, was D-Day for the invasion, and Lummus' unit was part of the initial wave that hit the beach. Lummus and the rest of the marines in the rifle platoon that he led then engaged in three weeks of intense fighting with the stubborn Japanese defenders. Of the action on March 8, Lieutenant Lummus' citation for gallantry reads:

Suddenly halted by a terrific concentration of hostile fire, [Lummus] *unhesitatingly moved forward of his front lines in an effort to neutralize the Japanese position. Although knocked to the ground when an enemy grenade exploded close by, he immediately recovered himself and,*

*again moving forward despite the intensified bar-
rage, quickly located, attacked, and destroyed the
occupied emplacement. Instantly taken under fire
by the garrison of a supporting pillbox and further
assailed by the slashing fury of hostile rifle fire, he fell
under the impact of a second enemy grenade but,
courageously disregarding painful shoulder wounds,
staunchly continued his heroic one-man assault
and charged the second pillbox, annihilating all
the occupants. Subsequently returning to his platoon position, he fearlessly traversed his lines
under fire, encouraging his men to advance and
directing the fire of supporting tanks against other
stubbornly holding Japanese emplacements. Held
up again by a devastating barrage, he again
moved into the open, rushed a third heavily fortified installation and killed the defending troops.
Determined to crush all resistance, he led his men
indomitably, personally attacking foxholes and
spider traps with his carbine and systematically
reducing the fanatic opposition until, stepping on
a land mine, he sustained fatal wounds.*

For his heroism on Iwo Jima, Jack Lummus was
posthumously awarded the Congressional Medal
of Honor.

Gifford Played, Talked a Good Game

Although the Giants of the 1950s and early '60s
were known for their great defensive teams, Frank
Gifford, the team's multi-threat back on offense, was
the team's best player. The team's 1952 first-round
pick was an All-America running back at USC.

Yet Gifford, who started his career as a two-way player, made his first impact on defense, where he was elected to the Pro Bowl in 1953 as a defensive back.

The young defensive star's athletic gifts were soon recognized and exploited by offensive coordinator Vince Lombardi. The post–World War II era of the NFL saw the phasing out of the two-way system in favor of a platoon system in which players specialized in either offense or defense. Gifford starred as the team's feature halfback and was a threat running, catching and even throwing the ball. With his skills showcased under Lombardi's scheme, Gifford earned league Most Valuable Player honors in 1956 as he led the NFL in yards from scrimmage (1422) with 819 yards rushing (5.2 average) and 603 yards receiving (11.8 average) on 51 receptions. He capped the season gaining 161 all-purpose yards from scrimmage and scored a touchdown in the team's 47–7 rout of Chicago in the NFL title game.

Gifford's string of seven consecutive Pro Bowl appearances ended in 1960, after he suffered a season-ending, and many feared career-ending, concussion when he was tackled by future Hall of Fame linebacker Chuck Bednarik of the Philadelphia Eagles. He sat out the 1961 season, then returned in 1962 as a flanker (wide receiver) and played for three more seasons, making the Pro Bowl in 1963 before retiring after the 1964 season.

Gifford who had his number 16 retired by the Giants, was elected into the Pro Football Hall of Fame in 1977 and enjoyed a successful broadcasting career, primarily with ABC Sports, after he retired. He was a member of the three-man broadcasting team of *Monday Night Football* for most of the first 20 years of the NFL's prime-time game. He was also a regular commentator on the network's Emmy Award–winning, Saturday-afternoon *Wide World of Sports*.

Y.A. Was A-OK

When quarterback Y.A. Tittle arrived in New York from San Francisco in 1961, he had already established himself as an All-Pro. What he was looking to do was play for a championship-caliber team, which the Giants were. In Tittle's first three years in New York, the Giants advanced to the NFL championship game each year but lost twice to the Packers and once to the Bears. Nearly a half-century after his retirement, Tittle still remains the most accomplished passer in team history. In 1962 and 1963, Tittle became the first quarterback to throw for more than 30 touchdowns in consecutive seasons, with 33 and a then-record 36, respectively. The 1963 touchdown total remained a league record until it was broken by Miami's Dan Marino, who threw for 48 touchdowns in 1984.

The greatest game in his Hall of Fame career came on October 28, 1962, against the Redskins at Yankee Stadium. The 36-year-old, former first-round pick out of LSU completed 27-of-39 passes for 505 yards and a record-tying seven touchdown passes. His favorite targets were receivers Del Shofner, who had 11 receptions for 269 yards with one touchdown, and Frank Gifford, who had four catches for 127 yards and a touchdown. Future Jets coach Joe Walton added six receptions for 63 yards and three touchdowns as the Giants built a 49–20 lead early in the fourth quarter. With his teammates urging that he go for the record eighth touchdown, Tittle demurred, saying it wouldn't be right to pile on the points, even though there was still plenty of time remaining in the game. New York eventually won 49–34. Tittle enjoyed three of his seven Pro Bowl seasons with the Giants and retired after the 1964 campaign. New York retired his number 14 jersey, and in 1971, Tittle was elected into the Pro Football Hall of Fame.

Few Kept Up With This Jones

By the mid-1960s, the great Giants teams had aged, and the Giffords, Tittles and Huffs had retired or been traded. Chants of "deee-fense" were no longer heard from the fans who still continued to pack Yankee Stadium on Sundays—the excitement was now coming from the other side of the line of scrimmage. The team had basically become a two-man show. Quarterback Fran Tarkenton, who they acquired from the Vikings, had found an enticing target in young new receiver Homer Jones.

A 6-foot-3, 220-pound wide out from Texas Southern University, Jones had the size of a tight end but speed second only to "Bullet Bob" Hayes of the Dallas Cowboys. Hayes had won the gold medal in the 100- and 200-meter sprints at the 1964 Olympics in Tokyo and was the world record holder in the 100.

It should be noted that Jones did beat Hayes on the track in college, in a 200-meter sprint at a National Association of Intercollegiate Athletics (NAIA) meet in 1962. "I may not be able to beat Bob," Jones once said, "but I'd be close enough to tap him on the shoulder."

In his first five years as a starter for the Giants from 1965 to 1969, Jones struck fear into defensive backs as he averaged 27.3, 21.8, 24.7, 23.5 and 17.7 yards per catch. He led the NFL in touchdown receptions in 1967 with 13 and was voted to the Pro Bowl following the 1967 and 1968 seasons. But it was what Jones did after he scored a touchdown that created his lasting legacy. Early in his career, Jones observed a teammate throw the football into the stands in a genuine display of emotion following a score. But at the time, the NFL actually fined players who did that. So looking for a gimmick to draw attention to himself, Jones decided that slamming the ball to the turf, or "spiking" the football as he called it, was an appropriate exclamation point to a touchdown, and in addition, he wouldn't be fined because the football didn't leave the field.

Needing to improve their anemic running game, New York traded Jones to Cleveland in 1970. The Browns needed a replacement for wide receiver Paul Warfield, who they had just traded to the Miami Dolphins. In return, Cleveland sent the Giants Ron Johnson, an All-American at Michigan who spent his rookie year backing up Leroy Kelly. Injuries cut short Jones' stint with the Browns, and he was traded to the St. Louis Cardinals but retired before the start of the 1971 season.

Even though his stay in Cleveland was brief, Jones did manage to make a bit of history. In the first-ever game on the league's new experiment called *Monday Night Football*, which was televised by ABC, Jones returned the second-half kickoff 98 yards for a touchdown—which was followed by the obligatory spike. Jones' legacy as a player is overshadowed by the explosion in popularity of his revolutionary end-zone celebrations. His 22.3 yards per reception for his career ranks first in NFL history for receivers with at least 200 career receptions. And, there are only two other players in league history with at least 200 catches and a 20-yards-per-catch average—Hayes and Warfield, who are both in the Pro Football Hall of Fame.

It has now been more than 40 years since Jones departed for Cleveland, and the Giants haven't come close to filling his shoes—but it's not for a lack of trying. They invested five first-round picks and seven second-round picks in wide receivers, yet only one of those premium picks were selected by fellow players to the Pro Bowl or named All-Pro, which is voted on by pro football writers who cover the sport. Despite four Super Bowl teams and three championships, the Giants didn't have another Pro Bowl receiver until 2009, when Steve Smith averaged 11.4 yards on 112 receptions.

Johnson Shines in the Darkest Era

After the franchise's glory years of the 1950s and early '60s, the Giants became the doormats of the NFL. From 1964 to 1980, it seemed like the team could do little right in the front office or on the field. Players acquired in trades who seemed fine on the surface went flat, and top-rated college draft picks were busts in the pros. So fans were pleasantly surprised when running back Ron Johnson actually lived up to his potential.

In 1967, Johnson capped a collegiate career at Michigan, where he set many school and Big Ten records. He earned All-America honors in 1968 and set a Division I single-game rushing mark of 347 yards against Wisconsin. Cleveland selected Johnson in the first round in 1969, but he spent his rookie season backing up Leroy Kelly, who was in the middle of a Hall of Fame career. The Giants shipped fleet receiver Homer Jones to the Browns in 1970 with the hope of adding some punch to their running game, and Johnson more than delivered as he rushed for a franchise record 1027 yards to lead the Giants to a 9–5 mark, their first winning record since 1963. Johnson's 1514 all-purpose yards from scrimmage that season was tops in the NFL.

He missed most of the 1971 season with injuries as the team slid to 4–10. He returned to form in 1972, gaining 1182 yards and adding 451 yards receiving, and his 14 touchdowns running and receiving was second to none in what would be the Giants' last winning season (8–6) until 1981. Johnson had a respectable outing in 1973, with 902 yards rushing, but injuries and declining talent in the huddle were hampering his production. He finally retired after the 1975 campaign at age 28.

During his off-seasons, Johnson began working for financial firms on Wall Street and eventually earned an MBA from Farleigh Dickenson. He has started several successful businesses and been involved in philanthropic endeavors in and around his community of Summit, New Jersey. Johnson's older brother, Alex, played 13 seasons in Major League Baseball (1964–76), including two with the Yankees (1974–75). The elder Johnson made the American League All-Star team in 1970, the same year he won the American League batting championship with a .329 average.

Give My Regards...

You can count All-Pros Fred Dryer and Fran Tarkenton among those who, when given the choice to stay in or leave New York and the neon lights of Broadway, opted for greener pastures out west. Dryer, a defensive end out of San Diego State, led the team in sacks each of his three years in New York (1969–71). He was traded to the Patriots in 1972, but before playing a down in New England, he was sent to the Rams (then based in Los Angeles), where he started for 10 years on one of the NFL's best defenses. In LA, he started dabbling in acting and eventually starred in the hit TV series *Hunter*, on which he hunted down criminals as an LAPD detective for seven seasons (1984–91).

Tarkenton, a former Georgia Bulldog, was a third-round pick of the expansion team Minnesota Vikings. He was the team's starter from 1961 to 1966, but he butted heads with coach Norm Van Brocklin and wanted out of Minnesota. In New York, his favorite receiving target was flanker Homer Jones, and the pair mastered the art of making something out of nothing. But after five roller-coaster seasons, four of which he was voted to the Pro Bowl, "Sir Francis" demanded to be traded, and the Giants sent him back to Minnesota, where he led the Vikings to three Super Bowls, all losses. Tarkenton retired following the 1978 season as the NFL's career leader in passing yards and touchdown passes.

Like his former teammate Dryer, Tarkenton enjoyed some high profile years after football. He was a commentator on *Monday Night Football* from 1979 to 1982 and a co-host, along with John Davidson and Cathy Lee Crosby, of the TV series *That's Incredible*, which ran from 1980 to 1983. Tarkenton was elected into the Pro Football Hall of Fame in 1986.

From Sheikh to Shank

Few kickers made a bigger impact with the Giants than Ali Haji-Sheikh. The ninth-round pick out of Michigan replaced Joe Danelo, who had a sub-par 1982 season and was sent packing after seven years in New York. Danelo converted less than half of his kicks from outside 30 yards, which turned out to be crucial in three games the team lost by a total of six points. The 1982 Giants, which were coming off their first playoff season in 17 years, went 4–5, a record that many fans felt should have been a 7–2 campaign and another trip to the post season.

In 1983, Sheikh came in and had a great rookie season. He set an NFL record for field goals, hitting 35-of-43 attempts, including a franchise-best 56-yarder. Sheikh not only made the All-Rookie team, but he was also voted to the Pro Bowl. Unfortunately, the kicker was the team's best offensive weapon that year, and the Giants finished 3–12–1.

In 1984, Sheikh injured his hamstring on his kicking leg, and his stats dropped significantly. The cheers of 1983 became boos. The injury continued to hamper his kicking, and "The Sheikh" was replaced midway through the 1985 season. He played for Atlanta in 1986 and was the kicker for the Washington Redskins in their championship season of 1987. Sheikh missed his only field-goal attempt of Super Bowl XXII against Denver, but he made all six of his extra-point tries in the Redskins' 42–10 win over the Broncos.

Simms Airs It Out

Quarterback Phil Simms entered the 1985 season with great anticipation. In 1984, the former number-one pick out of Moorhead State, Kentucky, was coming off his best career as a passer, throwing for a franchise record 4044 yards as the Giants advanced to the playoffs for the first time with

Simms at center. "Big Blue" came to Cincinnati on October 13 for a week-seven showdown against the Bengals. Cincinnati capitalized on early New York turnovers and grabbed a 21–3 halftime lead, which caused the Giants to abandon their running attack in the second half. Forced to throw, Simms had his greatest day as a passer. He completed 40-of-62 passes for a team record 513 yards. The seventh-year quarterback's favorite targets were tight end Mark Bavaro, who hauled in a team record 12 catches for 176 yards, and receiver Lionel Manuel, who had eight receptions for 111 yards. Unfortunately, Simms threw two interceptions and only one touchdown as the Giants lost 35–30.

Bavaro's Catch and Carry

When forecasting the 1985 NFL prospects, analysts concluded that one of the draft positions that was light on talent that year was tight end. Only one player was chosen at the position in each of the first two rounds. General manager George Young and coach Bill Parcells selected Mark Bavaro of Notre Dame in the fourth round and projected him to be, at least for his rookie season, a backup to the team's current starter Zeke Mowatt. But Mowatt was hurt during pre-season training camp that season and Bavaro, the 100th player selected in the draft, became—and remained—the team's starter until he retired six years later.

The 6-foot-4, 240-pound Bavaro, who earned All-America honors during his last season in South Bend, was a punishing blocker, which fit perfectly into the team's smash-mouth approach to moving the ball. When Simms dropped back to pass, he was a sure-handed receiver who instilled fear into defensive backs who tried to tackle him one-on-one. The play that best showcased the skills of the best tight end in franchise history came in a December 1986 showdown against their West Coast rivals in San Francisco.

The Giants, who trailed 17–0 at halftime, started a second-half comeback and cut the lead to 17–7. With the ball at midfield, quarterback Phil Simms dropped back and hit Bavaro at the San Francisco 40-yard line for what should have realistically been a 10, perhaps as much as 15, yard gain after he battled for a few extra yards. Bavaro was immediately hit by future Hall of Fame safety Ronnie Lott, then a second and third 49er. But they bounced off Bavaro as he continued to move down the field. A fourth, and then fifth, defender took their shots as the man who fans dubbed "Rambo"—for his Sylvester Stallone–type looks and physique—rambled down the field. Bavaro was finally tackled at the San Francisco 18-yard line. He picked up 32 yards and demoralized a total of seven 49er defenders who couldn't bring him down on the play. The Giants went on to cap the drive with a touchdown and eventually won the game 21–17.

Bavaro was a two-time Pro Bowler and started on the Giants first two Super Bowl championship teams. Unfortunately, injuries cut his career short, and he retired in 1991 at age 29. After taking a year off,

Bavaro returned for three more seasons with the Browns and Eagles. Years later, Simms fondly recalled the play against San Francisco as the signature moment of the team's first Super Bowl season.

Old Reliable

In sizing up the career of Hall of Fame linebacker Harry Carson, his teammates, coaches or opponents usually regaled his exploits in the same awe-inspiring manner as the teammate who played alongside him, Lawrence Taylor. While Taylor left everyone speechless as he wreaked havoc on opposing teams from sideline-to-sideline, Carson, the defensive unit's captain, played his inside linebacker position flawlessly as he earned Pro Bowl honors in nine of his 13 seasons from 1976 to 1988. The fourth-round pick out of South Carolina State University played middle linebacker early in his career when the Giants played a traditional 4–3 defense, and he stayed on the inside when they switched to a 3–4 scheme under coach Bill Parcells. Carson endured the final seasons of the pre-Parcells era and anchored a defensive unit that ranked with the league's best in the 1980s, culminating with the franchise's first Super Bowl championship season of 1986.

It remains one of the Pro Football Hall of Fame bylaw's greatest shortcomings that a player of Carson's caliber had to wait 15 years, until his last year of eligibility, before he garnered enough votes for enshrinement in 2006. Part of the oversight can be explained on Taylor getting all of the attention. If Taylor was Babe Ruth, then Carson was the Giants'

Lou Gehrig. Perhaps the greatest honor of Carson's career came before Super Bowl XXI when Parcells ordered his defensive captain to be the team's sole representative at midfield for the pre-game coin toss.

Walls' Second Cover's a Keeper

Defensive back Everson Walls played just three of his 13 seasons in the league with the Giants—the former Dallas Cowboy had most of his career highlights during his nine seasons in Big D. The one-time free agent out of Grambling State University led the NFL in interceptions three times, including his first two years in the league, and earned four trips to the Pro Bowl. But it was the way his rookie year ended that forever haunted him. In the famous 1981 NFC championship game at San Francisco, it was against Walls that Dwight Clark made his famous touchdown reception that gave the 49ers a 28–27 victory over Dallas. What made matters even worse for Walls was that a *Sports Illustrated* photographer was right near Clark in the end zone and took one of the most famous cover shots in the magazine's history. Walls became the reluctant co-star of the play known as "The Catch."

With new Dallas owner Jerry Jones and coach Jimmy Johnson committed to a youth movement, Walls was released and signed by the Giants before the 1990 season. It proved to be a good move, as Walls, who was moved from cornerback to safety, led the team in interceptions during the regular season and was a starter on the Giants thrilling last-second 20–19 win over Buffalo in Super Bowl XXV.

Once again, Walls was on the field at the climatic point of the game and leapt into the air to celebrate Scott Norwood's errant field-goal attempt to give New York the win. And once again, a *Sports Illustrated* photographer was there to capture the drama, and Walls was in the final picture. Only this time, he was the only one. And unlike his first appearance on the cover of *Sports Illustrated*, he made room for this one in the family scrapbook.

Ingram's Super Career Move(s)

During the 1990 season, wide receiver Mark Ingram finally started to show flashes of the skills that the Giants expected when they chose him with the last pick in the first round of the 1987 draft. Ingram's rookie season was curtailed by the NFL strike, and he missed half of the 1988 campaign with a broken collarbone. During the team's second Super Bowl run, the fourth-year receiver made a career-high 26 receptions for an impressive 19.2 yards per catch. Nevertheless, nobody was pleased with his career numbers.

Super Bowl XXV against Buffalo proved to be a tight battle beginning with the opening kickoff. The Giants opened the second half with a time-consuming drive and were facing a third-and-13 at the Buffalo 32 with the Bills leading 12–10. New York's quarterback Jeff Hostetler called a pass play—"half-right-62-comeback-dig"—in which Ingram was the key receiver. The former Michigan State Spartan ran an eight-yard "square-in" pattern and caught Hostetler's pass, but he was still five yards shy of the Buffalo 19, which is where he needed to get to. Ingram cut around defender Kirby Jackson, then turned up field and avoided a lunging linebacker Darryl Talley. Safety Mark Kelso also missed him, and Ingram headed toward the sideline before being grabbed by the ankles by James Williams. Ingram then twisted and lunged forward as he fell and picked up the first down at the Buffalo 18.

Five plays later, running back Ottis Anderson's scored on a one-yard run to give New York the lead, 17–12. Ingram's darting-and-diving maneuver kept alive what turned out to be a 14-play drive that consumed 9:29, the longest touchdown drive in Super Bowl history. The Giant's ball-control strategy worked perfect in their 20–19 win. New York's offense was on the field a record 40:33, which kept Buffalo's high-octane attack on the sidelines for all but 19:27.

Layover on Way to Super Bowl

Quarterbacks Phil Simms, Jeff Hostetler, Kerry Collins and Eli Manning have led the Giants to Super Bowl berths, yet more ex-Giants have played in the big game for other teams. Earl Morrall played for the Colts in Super Bowl III and V and was a member of Miami's two championship teams in the 1970s. Fran Tarkenton didn't make the playoffs during his six years in the Big Apple. His fortunes improved when he returned to Minnesota, leading the Vikings to three Super Bowls in four years, but they were clearly overmatched in three-straight losses to Miami, Pittsburgh and Oakland. Craig Morton came to the Giants from Dallas, where he led the Cowboys in a losing effort against Morrall and the Colts in Super Bowl V. After parts of three seasons in New York, he took Denver to its first Super Bowl against his old Cowboys teammates in Super Bowl XII. Kurt Warner led the Rams and their "Greatest Show on Turf" offense to two Super Bowl appearances in 1999 and 2001. After one season with the Giants (2005), he bounced around to a few teams before leading the Cardinals in a losing effort to the Steelers in Super Bowl XLIV.

Tyree's Miracle Catch

A dramatic ending is usually assured whenever a team from New York faces a team from New England with a championship on the line. This was equally the case in Super Bowl XLII when the Giants trailed New England 14–10 with just 1:15 left in the game. Just as a lightly regarded Bucky Dent became a New York hero with his dramatic home run in a sudden-death playoff with the Red Sox in 1978, backup receiver David Tyree stepped into the history books when the Giants broke the huddle facing a third down with five yards to go with the ball on the Patriots 44-yard line. The Patriots, who were 75 seconds from completing an undefeated season, were expecting a pass, and their fierce pass rush helped cause perhaps the greatest play in Super Bowl history.

At the snap of the ball in the shotgun formation, quarterback Eli Manning faced immediate pressure. He tried to avoid the rush, but the Patriots blocked every avenue. When three Patriots got a hold of Manning's jersey, it appeared as though they had the sack. But Manning somehow stayed on his feet and ducked under the arm of a Patriot defender before scrambling out into the open. In a split second that seemed to last forever, Manning spotted David Tyree and fired the ball toward his target as the two teams, the sellout crowd in University of Phoenix Stadium and millions of fans watching on television held their collective breath.

Tyree leapt into the air and caught the ball behind his head. But at the same time, Patriot defender Rodney Harrison was trying to tear the ball out of his hands. Through sheer will, Tyree pressed the ball to his helmet with one hand and managed to pull the ball in for the reception. The play covered 32 yards and gave New York a first down on the New England 24-yard line with 59 seconds left. Four plays later, Plaxico Burress scored the game-winning touchdown, and the Giants won their third Super Bowl.

Tragedy Avoided

A little known fact from the Giants Super Bowl victory is that it nearly turned into a tragedy. Kurt William Havelock had applied to the city of Phoenix, Arizona, for a liquor license in order to open up a bar to profit from the crowds that were set to descend on the city for the 2007 Super Bowl. However, when Havelock was denied his permit, he became very angry with city officials and threatened to shoot people at random at the Super Bowl.

Havelock sent letters to the media informing them of his complaints and his intentions to shoot up the Super Bowl. He even went as far as to purchase an AR-15 assault rifle with 200 rounds of ammunition, and then he drove out to the stadium but decided at the last minute not to go through with his sadistic plans. After telling some family members of his plans, he turned himself into the police and was arrested. The incident was only made public after the Giants had won the Super Bowl.

New York Jets

Two Epic Games, One Coach

Most football historians agree that the two most important games in pro football history are the Colts overtime win over the Giants in the 1958 NFL championship game, and the Jets upset of the Colts 10 years later in Super Bowl III. That both games involved New York teams and the Baltimore Colts is not the only common thread. The other is that the winning coach in both games was the same man, Wilbur "Weeb" Ewbank. It says something about the man's low-key approach to his profession that so little is made of this accomplishment, or that he helped mold the careers of two future Hall of Fame quarterbacks: John Unitas and Joe Namath.

Ewbank was born in Richmond, Indiana, in 1907. He was a star at Miami University, Ohio, where one of his teammates was Paul Brown. He began his coaching career at the high school level and eventually coached basketball at his alma mater before joining the navy in World War II, where he was a physical fitness instructor along with his old college teammate, Brown.

After the war, Ewbank became the head coach at Washington University in St. Louis for two seasons before moving east to Brown University in the Ivy League, where he was the backfield coach. One of his players was a young kid from Brooklyn who became the starting quarterback. But unlike Unitas and Namath, young Joe Paterno never made it as a pro quarterback, though he didn't do too badly as a coach himself. One year later, Brown offered Ewbank a position with the Cleveland Browns. The Browns were among the elite franchises in pro football, so it was only natural that Baltimore owner Carroll Rosenbloom looked to the Cleveland staff when he needed a new coach in 1954. Again, Brown recommended his old friend Ewbank.

Weeb Makes Colts and Jets Champs

In Baltimore, Ewbank inherited a losing team, and it took a few seasons to turn the franchise around. There was another future NFL great on Ewbank's roster in his early years in Baltimore who, like Paterno, made the Hall of Fame as a coach but not a player. His name was Don Shula. The Colts finally had a winning season in 1957 and a year later won the NFL championship with a thrilling 23–17 win over the Giants at Yankee Stadium. The sellout crowd on hand and the rest of the nation watching on television watched as Ewbank's Colts, guided by Unitas, tied the score at the end of regulation with a picture-perfect, two-minute drive, then won the championship in the league's first-ever overtime game (up until the 1970s, the NFL didn't have overtime games except for the playoffs and championship games). The Colts beat the Giants for the championship again in 1959, but then the team went into a slide and had losing seasons in 1961 and 1962, so Ewbank was fired.

He was immediately hired by Sonny Werblin of the New York franchise of the AFL, which had just changed its name from Titans to Jets. A year later, the Jets signed Namath, who had starred for two seasons for Bear Bryant at Alabama. Ewbank began to bring in players to surround his young gun-slinging quarterback—who set a pro football record for yards in a season (4007) in 1967—and a year later, the Jets were AFL champions. As he had a decade earlier, Ewbank ignored the pre-game forecast by the odds makers and constructed an offensive game plan that successfully attacked the Colts defense, which was considered the best of its generation. Injuries to Namath played a key role in the Jets inability to repeat as champions, and the team slid to mediocrity by 1972, when Ewbank retired.

The architect of victory in pro football's two most significant games earned his place alongside the two great field generals who engineered the victories in the Pro Football Hall of Fame. Ewbank's players in the Hall of Fame include Art Donovan, Jim Parker, John Unitas, Raymond Berry, Lenny Moore, Gino Marchetti and Don Shula from the Colts,

and Joe Namath, John Riggins and Don Maynard
with the Jets.

Everyone but the Jets Were Stunned

The Jets were 18-point underdogs when they took
the field against the Colts in Super Bowl III at the
Orange Bowl. The young AFL champions had just
completed their best season with an 11–3 record.
They were facing the Baltimore Colts, who had lost
just once in 14 games and boasted the NFL best
units on both sides of the ball. And to boot, the Colts
did it all with a backup, Earl Morrall, as their starting quarterback for most of the season. They lost
future Hall of Famer John Unitas early in the season
to an arm injury. Although Unitas had been cleared
by team doctors to play, Shula determined that he
would only be used only if Morrall got hurt or in an
emergency situation. But not everyone in Miami
was in awe of the Colts. After fielding patronizing
questions for a few days, Jets quarterback Joe
Namath made headlines from coast to coast when
he declared, "We're going to win. I guarantee it."

Conventional wisdom dictated that if Namath
and his teammates were going to succeed, he'd have
to have a great day passing to his fleet receivers Don
Maynard and George Sauer. Not surprisingly, the
Colts defense was ready for him. Only Namath,
until that day not given his due as a field general,
kept the Baltimore defense off-stride throughout the
game with a ball-control running attack. Full back
Matt Snell gained 121 yards on 30 carries, including
a four-yard touchdown run in the second quarter

that gave New York a 6–0 lead. The rifle-armed quarterback enjoyed a more modest day, completing 17-of-28 passes for 206 yards with no interceptions.

Meanwhile, Morrall, the NFL's Most Valuable Player that season, had a career-worst day. He completed just 6-of-17 passes for 71 yards and three interceptions. Despite having the ball in Jets territory six times, they had no points. Namath and Snell continued to gain ground and eventually held the ball for 36:10 as the Jets built a 16–0 lead before Baltimore coach Don Shula acknowledged that it was now an "emergency situation" and finally replaced Morrall with Unitas in the fourth quarter. It was too little, too late, however, as the Jets beat the Colts 16–7 and placed the AFL on equal footing with the senior league.

Record-setting Boot

It was a given that, as the Jets entered the 1969 season to defend their Super Bowl crown, they would rely heavily on the right arm of quarterback Joe Namath. Few could have anticipated that, by the season's end, the team's top highlight would come courtesy of the right foot of that year's 13th-round draft pick, Steve O'Neal.

The rookie punter out of Texas A&M did not have football on his mind when he left high school. His athletic scholarship to College Station was for track and field. His membership on the Aggie football roster was sheer accident. As O'Neal was warming up for practice in the summer of 1966 near the football team's practice field, an overthrown ball landed near him. Rather than throw it back, O'Neal kicked the ball back. The kick was so impressive that he was asked to boot a few more and eventually was invited to become the team's punter. Once again, football was not O'Neal's primary concern when he graduated A&M in the spring of 1969—his career goal was to attend dental school.

But he made the Jets, who had just scored a historic win over the Baltimore Colts in Super Bowl III, so dental school had to wait—his entry into the NFL record book came much sooner. In a week-two game in Denver, the Jets were backed up to their one-yard line when O'Neal entered with the punting unit. With his heels near the back line of the end zone, O'Neal took the snap and booted the ball high into the air. To Denver's rookie punt returner Billy Thompson, who was standing near midfield, it looked more like a perfectly thrown spiral pass, only it was way over his head. The ball traveled 75 yards in the air and started to roll toward the Broncos end zone. Thompson, who was the AFL's top punt return in 1969, began running the ball down but it just kept rolling. Despite Thompson's efforts, the ball eventually rolled out of bounds at the Denver one-yard line, giving O'Neal a still unequalled 98-yard punt.

The record-setting boot is also the longest punt for net yards, since, if the ball had bounced into the end zone, it would have been a touchback, and the Broncos would have started on their own 20.

The punt was the highlight of the game, which the Jets lost 21–19. They finished the season 10–4 but lost to eventual Super Bowl champion Kansas City in the playoffs. Thompson, whose inability to stop the punt enabled the record, became an All-Pro safety for the Broncos famed "Orange Crush" defensive unit that powered the team to Super Bowl XII. O'Neal spent four seasons with the Jets and one with New Orleans, before completing his dental studies and becoming a full-time dentist.

Namath Outguns Unitas

Perhaps the only thing lacking from the Jets win over the Colts in Super Bowl III was a healthy John Unitas starting at center for Baltimore. The 10-time Pro Bowler and future Hall of Famer hurt his throwing arm early in the 1968 season and was only available in an emergency situation. When coach Don Shula finally turned to Unitas in the fourth quarter, the Colts trailed 16–0.

When the AFL merged with the NFL in 1970, the Colts moved to the new AFC East Division, which also had the Bills, Patriots and Jets. Namath suffered through two injury-plagued seasons, missing 8-of-28 games. There were still more than 10 players on both sides who played in the historic meeting four years earlier, but both teams had slid to mediocrity. The matchup fans were looking for eventually took place when the Jets played the Colts on September 24, 1972, at Memorial Stadium in Baltimore.

After the teams exchanged punts on their first possessions, Namath—who used to keep a photo of Unitas over the headboard of his bed as a boy—took to the air and hit receiver Eddie Bell on a 65-yard scoring pass that gave New York a quick 6–0 lead. Later in the quarter, Unitas showed some flash when he connected with Sam Havrilak on a 40-yard flea flicker, and the first quarter ended with Baltimore ahead 7–6. Two Colts field goals increased their lead to 13–6 in the second quarter, and then their defense got stung for three touchdowns in 89 seconds. Namath threw touchdown passes to John Riggins (67 yards), Don Maynard (28 yards) and Rich Caster (10 yards). If that wasn't enough excitement, a Don McCauley 97-yard touchdown return kept Colts fans from leaving early as the Jets led at halftime, 27–20.

Both teams cooled off during the break as New York just managed a field goal in the third quarter to increase its lead to 30–20. McCauley's one-yard touchdown run and Jim O'Brien's extra point cut the Baltimore deficit to 30–27. On the ensuing possession, Namath found Caster for a 79-yard score. Unitas then marched the Colts down the field and culminated a 10-play drive with a 21-yard touchdown pass to Tom Matte. Undaunted, Namath answered with an 80-yard bomb to Caster. Kicker Bobby Howfield's extra point gave the Jets a 44–34 victory.

Namath threw 28 passes and completed 15 on what was his greatest day throwing the football. He threw just one interception against six touchdowns for 496 yards, both career highs. Unitas threw for 376 yards, making 26-of-45 passes with two touchdowns and no interceptions. Their combined 872 yards passing set an NFL record.

All-Pro Hill Missing from Hall of Fame

There is no question as to who was the greatest offensive lineman in Jets history. That distinction goes to Winston Hill, who was the starting left tackle from 1963 to 1976. In between, Hill started a club record 174 consecutive games and was an AFL All-Star and an AFC Pro Bowl selection eight times—seven consecutive from 1967 to 1973. What the "Gang Green" faithful want to know most of all is why Hill, who was named to the AFL's All-Time Team, is not enshrined in the Pro Football Hall of Fame.

The 6-foot-5, 270-pound lineman out of Texas Southern was selected by the Baltimore Colts in the 11th round of the 1963 draft. Baltimore had drafted All-American offensive left tackle Bob Vogel of Ohio State in the first round, and on the right side Jim Parker was in the middle of his Hall of Fame career—so Hill elected into join the Jets of the AFL. Hill became a starter in his rookie year and was an AFL All-Star his second. Hill began his streak of seven consecutive All-Star and Pro Bowl appearances in 1967, which was also New York's first winning season. Perhaps a significant reason quarterback Joe Namath was so confident that the Jets would beat Baltimore in Super Bowl III was because he had Hill protecting his blind side. On Super Bowl Sunday, Hill and guard Bob Talamini dominated their Colts counterparts, who were the top defensive unit in the NFL that season. The duo protected Namath and opened holes for Matt Snell, who picked up 121 yards on 30 carries.

Hill's exclusion from the Hall of Fame makes no sense, especially when you consider that fellow AFL alumnus Art Shell (Raiders) and Ron Mix (Chargers), both of whom appeared in eight All-Star games and Pro Bowls, were enshrined more than 20 years ago. In retirement, Hill has run a successful restaurant in Denver called Winston Hill's Ribs & Stuff. It's ironic that the restaurant is open Monday through Saturday and closed on Sundays, which was the only day that Hill never took off as a football player.

Young Guns Beat Old Guns

Miami's Dan Marino may have been the most prolific passer of his era, but in Ken O'Brien, the Jets had a signal caller who led the team to three playoff appearances. Although O'Brien, like the rest of the quarterbacks in the league, lacked Marino's arm strength, he had some juice in his gun as well. In 1985, the two former 1983 first-round picks put on an aerial show that garnered comparisons to the 1972 shootout between Joe Namath and John Unitas. On November 10 at the Orange Bowl, O'Brien was 26-of-43 for a career high 393 yards, but threw only two touchdowns. Marino was 21-of-37 for 362 yards. His third touchdown pass, a 50-yarder to Mark Duper, came with less than a minute to play and gave Miami a 21–17 win.

The 1985 meeting turned out to be a primer. During a game on September 21, 1986, at the Meadowlands, Miami's future Hall of Fame quarterback completed 30-of-50 passes for 448 yards and six touchdowns. O'Brien answered with 29-of-43 for 479 yards and four touchdowns. All four touchdown strikes were to Wesley Walker, including a 21-yard strike that tied the score at 45 late in regulation, and a 43-yarder in overtime for a 51–45 win. Walker was O'Brien's favorite target in that game, making six receptions for 196 yards. The 929 combined yards passing by O'Brien and Marino bested the previous mark of 872 yards set by Namath and Unitas and remains a record to this day.

Buffalo Bills

New York's Team of the '60s

The Buffalo Bills have been the butt of many jokes since losing four consecutive Super Bowls from 1990 to 1993, but the franchise does boast two championships from their days in the AFL. Under coach Lou Saban and led on the field by quarterback Jack Kemp, the Bills were the class of the AFL, and perhaps all of professional football, in 1964 and 1965. Buffalo's '64 championship team was exceptional—the Bills had the league's top-scoring offense and stingiest defense. Kemp and running back "Cookie" Gilchrist were perennial All-Stars, while linebacker Mike Stratton, an eventual six-time Pro Bowler, anchored a defense that allowed the fewest points both championship seasons. With Gilchrist grinding out yards on the ground that first championship season, Kemp hooked up with receiver Elbert Dubenion, who had a career season with 42 receptions for 1139 yards—an astonishing 27.1 yards per catch—and 10 touchdowns. Buffalo won its first nine games en route to a 12–2 season and beat San Diego for the AFL title, 20–7.

Gilchrist was traded during the offseason, but Buffalo was strong enough to repeat as Kemp earned co-MVP honors, and the team finished 10–3–1. Again, they defeated San Diego in the championship game, this time by a score of 23–0. By 1966, talk of merging the NFL and AFL was underway by the owners, and it was agreed the leagues' respective champions would meet to decide the first-ever championship of professional football (the term "Super Bowl" had yet to be coined). But Saban left the Bills after the second championship to coach at the University of Maryland, and injuries and age began to take their toll. The 1966 Bills won the Eastern Division for the third consecutive season but lost the AFL championship game to Kansas City, 31–7.

The team was mired in mediocrity for most of the next decade, but how many fans realized it at the time, or even know now, that from 1960 to 1981, Buffalo was the most successful of New York's three professional football teams? The Giants lost all three NFL title games they played in from 1961 to 1963, and the Jets won their lone AFL crown in 1968. The Bills, on the other hand, won two of the three AFL championship games they played in, made eight trips to the playoffs and had 13 winning seasons. They were also the only New York team to earn a playoff berth during the 1970s.

One Tough Cookie

To say that Carlton Chester "Cookie" Gilchrist marched to the beat of his own drum is an understatement. He marched to the beat of his own *parade*, often leaving his teammates, coaches and management exasperated. But on the field, the 6-foot-1, 230-pound fullback, who never played a down of college football, earned a reputation as one of the great running backs of his—and any other—era.

Gilchrist was a star runner during his junior year for Har-Brack High School in Natrona, Pennsylvania, but because he turned 19 during his senior season in 1954, he was ineligible for high school ball. Paul Brown, the head coach of the Cleveland Browns at the time, offered the teen sensation a contract with the Browns, but the NFL stepped in and refused to allow the high school direct-to-pro transition. However, because Gilchrist had accepted the Browns offer, he was also barred from playing college ball. So he went to Canada, where he played in the CFL. Gilchrist set team and league marks as he starred for four teams over seven seasons. But as impressive as his exploits were on the Canadian gridiron, they offered neither the fame nor the fortune accorded to players in American pro football leagues.

Finally, in 1962 at age 27, Gilchrist signed a contract with Buffalo of the AFL. Gilchrist made an immediate impact, leading the league in rushing (1150) and touchdowns (13) and became the first back in the league's short history to run for 1000 yards. He led the league in touchdowns again in 1963 and 1964 but fell just shy of the 1000-yard barrier, with 979 and 981 yards, respectively. Gilchrist led the league in touchdowns and was named to the AFL All-Star team in all three of his seasons in Buffalo. In 1963, he set an AFL and pro football single-game rushing record when he ran for 243 yards against the Jets before a hometown crowd at War Memorial Stadium.

As good as Gilchrist was, he was a headache to the coaching staff and management in the sense that he had a higher appreciation for his talent than he believed the Bills did. Everything came to a head during a 1964 regular-season game against the then-Boston Patriots. Gilchrist became upset with a pass-oriented game plan and took himself out of the game and later refused to return to the field. The Bills lost, and coach Lou Saban cut Gilchrist after the game. But quarterback Jack Kemp interceded on his teammate's behalf, and Saban took Gilchrist back after the player made a public apology. The Bills finished the season 12–2, and Gilchrist ran for 122 yards on 16 carries as Buffalo defeated San Diego in the AFL championship game, 20–7.

Gilchrist was traded to Denver after the season and again made the All-Star team in 1965. But problems with the front office in Denver caused him to be traded to Miami, where he seldom played because of injuries. He was back in Denver for the 1967 campaign, but played just one game. At age 32, the career of this victim of circumstance and hubris was over.

Kalsu Walked the Walk

James Robert "Bob" Kalsu was, if you can excuse the quaint term, "Everybody's All-American." He was an excellent athlete, a devout Roman Catholic, a loyal friend with a great sense of humor and a devoted husband and father. He grew up in Del City, Oklahoma, where he was a star athlete in high school and was recruited to Oklahoma University (OU) by legendary coach Bud Wilkinson. Kalsu justified Wilkinson's faith by earning All-America honors as an offensive tackle his senior season of 1967. Kalsu married Jan Darrow, who he met in 1966, a few weeks after Oklahoma won the Orange Bowl his senior season.

At OU, Kalsu enrolled in the Reserve Officers' Training Corps (ROTC) program and was commissioned a second lieutenant upon graduation. He was then drafted in the eighth round by the Buffalo Bills. He would have been selected higher, but many teams were scared off by his military commitment. Kalsu made the Bills' final roster and started nine games at right guard in 1968 and was named the team's Rookie of the Year. But he was called to active duty in March 1969 and shortly after was sent to Vietnam.

By the summer of 1970, Kalsu was already the father of a baby girl, and Jan was expecting their second child. But on July 21, Kalsu was among the men in his unit who were killed from enemy bombardment. Two days later, back in Oklahoma, Jan gave birth to a boy, Robert Todd Kalsu. Upon receiving news of her husband's death, Jan left the hospital but not before she changed her son's birth certificate to James Robert Kalsu Jr.

Although he played just one season in Buffalo, Kalsu is still remembered fondly by his teammates and coaches. The Bills acknowledged Kalsu's time with the team and his wartime sacrifice with a joint football-and-military display that hangs on the team's Wall of Fame in the lobby of Ralph Wilson Stadium.

Miami Had the Oranges, But Buffalo Had "The Juice"

O. J., that is. The Buffalo Bills made two acquisitions prior to the 1969 season that, on their face, looked promising for the future. First, they signed John Rauch as their new head coach. Rauch, who had been fired by the Raiders, had gone 25–3 in his last two seasons with the Silver and Black. The second promising decision was drafting 1968 Heisman Trophy–winner Orenthal James Simpson out of USC with their first-round pick. In a decision that rivaled the Coca-Cola executive who gave us the ill-fated "New Coke," Rauch tried to use Simpson as a multipurpose back and flanker. Simpson gained less than 1000 yards from scrimmage in each of his first three seasons. Rauch got canned after two seasons with a 7–20–1 record. The "O. J. as a decoy" madness continued in 1971 under former defensive backfield coach Harvey Johnson. Johnson, who was an interim coach in 1968, was 1–13 in 1971 before he too got canned.

With Simpson's career wallowing in mediocrity, owner Ralph Wilson rehired coach Lou Saban, who led the Bills to their two AFL titles in 1964 and 1965. Saban restored Simpson to his natural position of running back and built the Bills offense around the player many believed to be among the best in the game back when he entered the league. Among the coach's top priorities was assembling an offensive line. Tackles Dave Foley and Donnie Green and guard Reggie McKenzie started most of 1972 as Simpson led the NFL in rushing with 1251 yards. A year later, they added center Mike Montler and guard Joe DeLamielleure to form a line that rivaled the men up front for the defending champion Miami Dolphins.

In 1973, the unit dubbed "The Electric Company" opened up holes and turned on "The Juice" as Simpson set a single-season rushing record of 2003 yards. Simpson was the only runner during pro football's 14-game seasons (1961–77) who broke the 2000-yard mark. McKenzie and Foley were voted to the Pro Bowl in 1973, and DeLamielleure, who went to five Pro Bowls with the Bills, was elected into the Pro Football Hall of Fame in 2003.

While Miami's more balanced offensive attack, which featured the running of Larry Csonka, Mercury Morris and Jim Kiik, powered the Dolphins to three consecutive Super Bowls and two championships, Simpson was the only offensive weapon in Buffalo. Nevertheless, the Electric Company's superb run blocking enabled the franchise's greatest runner to lead the NFL in rushing four times from 1972 to 1976. The Juice and the Electric Company ran against the vaunted Miami "No Name Defense" 16 times during the 1970s and he gained a very respectable 1117 yards on 240 carries for a 4.9 average. However, despite the future Hall of Famer's success, Miami won all 16 games.

Levy's Career Mirrors Grant's

Former head coach Marv Levy has several things in common with former Vikings coach Bud Grant. Both were multi-sport stars in college, with the Chicago native Levy earning varsity letters in football, basketball and track at Coe College in Iowa. Like Grant, Levy's first crack at coaching came north of the border in the CFL, where he won two CFL championships with the Montreal Alouettes to Grant's four. In the NFL, both came to losing franchises but soon turned them into consistent winners. Unfortunately, they also share a distinction of both losing all four Super Bowls their teams participated in. And Levy, like Grant, remains the winningest coach in the history of his respective franchise and earned his place, alongside several of his players, in the Pro Football Hall of Fame.

Unlike Minnesota, which never held a lead and never covered the point-spread in any of its four Super Bowl losses, the Bills' loss to the Giants was a nail-biter and remains one of the greatest championship games in NFL history. And though they led at halftime, 13–3, in their fourth and final trip to the big game, it still ended up being a 33–13 loss to Dallas.

Reich Has the Right Stuff

One of the least stressful jobs on a football team is that of backup quarterback. He's seldom used, but nonetheless he must be prepared in case the starter goes down. Bills quarterback Frank Reich had thrown just 258 passes in his seven years as an understudy when he filled in as the starter for injured Jim Kelly in a 1992 AFC Wild Card game against the Houston Oilers at Rich Stadium. But in the first half, Houston quarterback Warren Moon was everything Reich was not—hot. The future Hall of Famer threw four touchdown passes as the Oilers went into the locker room at halftime with a dominating 28–3 lead. A third consecutive AFC championship for the Bills seemed a long shot as the second half got underway.

Then on the Bills' first possession of the second half, Reich was intercepted by Bubba McDowell, who ran 58 yards for a touchdown. With the point after, Buffalo now trailed 35–3. Within minutes, there was a traffic jam outside the stadium as many of the 75,000 headed home. Who could blame the Buffalo fans? No team in history had ever come back from a 32-point deficit in the second half. But Reich had faced seemingly insurmountable odds before in a big game. In his senior year at Maryland in 1984, Reich and the Terrapins overcame a record 31–0 halftime deficit against Miami on the road. At least now he didn't have to contend with a hostile crowd at the Orange Bowl.

Buffalo's first trip to the end zone was by Kenneth Davis, who capped a 10-play drive with a one-yard run. Then kicker Steve Christie recovered the ensuing onside kick, and Reich took command. He calmly directed the offense as he connected first with Don Beebe and then hooked up with Andre Reed for three more touchdowns. The Buffalo defense, which was helpless in the first half, stuffed the Oilers repeatedly and even intercepted Moon to set up another touchdown. Amazingly, the Bills went ahead 38–35 with just under three minutes to play. With seconds left in regulation, the Oilers' Al Del Greco tied the score with a 26-yard field-goal kick to send the game into overtime.

Houston won the toss and elected to receive. But on the first possession, Nate Odomes intercepted Moon and a facemask penalty by the Oilers gave Buffalo the ball at the Houston 20. Three plays later, Christie converted a field goal from 32 yards out to give Buffalo the win in what remains the greatest comeback in NFL history.

Chapter Nine

Stamps of Approval

Since the 1980s, the U.S. Postal Service has periodically honored famous American athletes by issuing stamps in their honor. The only requirement is that the athlete must have been dead for at least 10 years. Below is a list of athletes either from New York state or who played for or coached New York teams or universities.

Baseball
    Jackie Robinson (1982)
    Babe Ruth (1983)
    Lou Gehrig (1989)
    Roger Maris (1999)
    Eddie Collins (2000)
    Christy Mathewson (2000)
    Satchel Paige (2000)
    Roy Campanella (2006)
    Hank Greenberg (2006)
    Mickey Mantle (2006)
    Mel Ott (2006)

Basketball
    (*none*)

Boxing

Joe Louis (1993)
Jack Dempsey (1998)
Rocky Marciano (1999)
Sugar Ray Robinson (2006)

Football

Jim Thorpe (1984)
George Halas (1997)
Vince Lombardi (1997)
Glenn "Pop" Warner (1997)
Jim Crowley (1998)
Elmer Layden (1998)
Harry Stuhldreher (1998)
Red Grange (2003)

Hockey

(*none*)

Olympics

Eddie Eagan (1990)
Ray Ewry (1990)

Notes on Sources

Book Sources

Carroll, Bob, Michael Gershman, David Neft, and John Thorn. *Total Football II: The Official Encyclopedia of the National Football League.* New York: HarperCollins, 1999.

Creamer, Robert. *Babe: A Legend Comes to Life.* New York: Simon & Schuster, 1974.

D'Antonio, Michael. *Forever Blue: The True Story of Walter O'Malley, Baseball's Most Controversial Owner, and the Dodgers of Brooklyn and Los Angeles.* New York: Riverhead Books, 2009.

Hillenbrand, Laura. *Unbroken: A World War II Story of Survival, Resilience and Redemption.* New York: Random House, 2010.

Kahn, Roger. *A Flame of Pure Fire: Jack Dempsey and the Roaring '20s.* New York: Houghton Mifflin Harcourt, 1999.

Louis, Joe, Edna Rust, and Art Rust Jr. *Joe Louis: My Life.* New York: Harcourt Brace Jovanovich, 1978.

MacArthur, Douglas. *Reminiscences.* New York: McGraw Hill, 1964.

Roberts, Randy. *Jack Dempsey: The Manassa Mauler.* Baton Rouge: Louisiana State University Press, 1979.

Strasen, Marty. *New York Giants: Yesterday and Today.* Illinois: West Side Publishing, 2009.

Print Sources

Baseball Digest

The Des Moines Register

Los Angeles Times

Middletown Record

New York Times

Newsday

Pittsburgh Post-Gazette

The Ring

Sports Illustrated

Time Magazine

USA Today

Web Sources

Baseball Almanac.com: www.baseball-almanac.com

Baseball-Reference.com: www.baseball-reference.com

Baseball Biography Project: bioproj.sabr.org

Basketball-Reference.com: www.basketball-reference.com

BoxRec: boxrec.com

Casey Stengel Official Site: www.caseystengel.com

CBS Sports.com: www.cbssports.com

Christy Mathewson Official Site: www.christymathewson.com

DatabaseOlympics.com: www.databaseolympics.com

Joe DiMaggio Official Site: www.joedimaggio.com

ESPN Classic: www.ESPN.go.com

Football-Reference.com: www.football-reference.com

For What They Gave on Saturday Afternoon: forwhattheygaveonsaturdayafternoon.com

Greater Buffalo Sports Hall of Fame: www. buffalosportshallfame.com

Hockey-Reference.com: www.hockey-reference.com

International Boxing Hall of Fame: www.ibhof.com

National Wrestling Hall of Fame Dan Gable Museum: www.wrestlingmuseum.org

NBA.com: www.nba.com

NHL.com: www.nhl.com

The Official Site of Pop Warner Little Scholars: www.popwarner.com

Walter O'Malley Official Site: www.walteromalley.com

Professional Researchers Association: profootballresearchers.org

Secretariat Official Site: www.secretariat.com

Sports Illustrated.com: sportsillustrated.cnn.com

Syracuse University Official Athletic Site: www. suathletics.com

St. Bonaventure Official Athletic Site: www. gobonnies.com

Swim the Channel: swimthechannel.net

Ed Maloney

Ed Maloney has been a sportswriter for almost longer than he can remember. He spent his first 15 years in the business as a staff editor and online producer at New York–Long Island *Newsday*. He also spent 16 years as a staff editor and feature columnist at London Publishing, which produced *The Ring, KO* and *World Boxing* magazines, before moving to Florida, where he ran the pro football and boxing channels at CBS SportsLine and eventually assumed similar duties with the official web site of the San Francisco 49ers. He is a graduate of Niagara University with a degree in English, majoring in communications. Not content to just write the news, he once made headlines when he helped snag and haul in a nine-foot, 500-pound bull shark off a dock on Tampa Bay

J. Alexander Poulton

J. Alexander Poulton is a writer, photographer and genuine sports enthusiast. He's even willing to admit he has "called in sick" during the broadcasts of major sports events so that he can get in as much viewing as possible.

He has earned a BA in English literature and a graduate diploma in journalism, and has over 25 sports books to his credit, including books on hockey, soccer, golf and the Olympics.